The Complete UNOFFICIAL Encyclopedia to The Sopranos

By: Kristina Benson

The Complete Unofficial Encyclopedia to The Sopranos

ISBN: 978-1-60332-048-1

Edited By: Brooke Winger

Copyright© 2008 Equity Press. No part of this publication may be reproduced, stored in a retrieval system, or transmitted in any form or by any means (electronic, mechanical, photocopying, recording or otherwise) without either the prior written permission of the publisher or a license permitting restricted copying in the United States or abroad.

The scanning, uploading and distribution of this book via the internet or via any other means without the permission of the publisher is illegal and punishable by law. Please purchase only authorized electronic editions, and do not participate in or encourage piracy of copyrighted materials.

Trademarks: All trademarks are the property of their respective owners. Equity Press is not associated with any product or vender mentioned in this book.

Printed in the United States of America

Table of Contents

The Sopranos Encyclopedia 10
   Soprano, Tony 12
   Soprano, Carmela 13
   Soprano, Meadow Mariangela 14
   Soprano, Anthony Junior, a.k.a. AJ 15
   Soprano, Livia 15
   Anxiety Attacks 16
   Animals 16
   Moltisanti, Christopher 17
   Rabkin, Herman "Hesh" 18
   Pelstin, Irina 18
   Melfi, Jennifer, MD 19
   Vesuvio 20
   Triborough Towers Garbage 20
   Father Phil 20
   Stugots 21
   Aprile, Giacomo "Jackie Sr" 21
   Filone, Brendan: 21
   Comley Trucks 22
   Satriale's 22
   Bada Bing 23
   Teittleman, Shlomo 23
   Ariel 23
   Masada 24
   Golem 24
   Piocosta, Jeremy 25
   Meadowlands 25
   Petrulio, Fabian "Febby" 25
   Hawthorne, Nathanial 25
   Lupertazzi Crime Family 26
   Down Neck 26
   Cusamano, Bruce, MD 27
   Santini, Richard: 27
   La Cerva, Liz 28
   Safir, Amy 29
   Francesco, Tina 29
   Testa, Matt 30
   Dolan, JT 30

Massarone Construction 31
"You Bark, I Bite" 31
Ramsey Sports and Outdoors 31
Kirilenko, Svetlana 32
Baccalieri, Dominica 33
Cammarata, Brian 33
Blundetto, Quintina Pollio 34
Blundetto, Tony 34
De Angelis, Hugh 36
De Angelis, Mary Pellegrino 37
Giglione, Tom 38
Giglione, Barbara Soprano 38
Moltisani, Joanne 39
DiMeo, Domenico Ercoli "Eckley" 40
Palmice, Mikey "Grab Bag" 40
Joseph "Beppy" Sasso 42
Soprano, Corrano John "Junior" 42
Alfie 44
Annunziata, Perry 45
Bevilaqua, Mathew 45
Blundetto, Pat 46
Caporale, Corky 47
Cortese, Frankie 47
De La Rosa, Peter "Petey" 48
DiBartolo, Cary 48
Giarizzo, Gaetano 49
Gervasi, Burt 49
Gismonte, Sean 50
Georgie 51
Ianucci, Corky 52
Moltisanti, Richard "Dickie" 52
Zancone, James "Murmur" 53
Cestone, Gigi 53
Cippolina, "Big" Frank 54
Gaeta, Peter "Beansie" 55
Greco, Dante 55
Coniglio, Bobby 56
DiGioia, Corky 56
Dogsy 56

Donny K	57
Molinaro, Jason	57
Carlo Renzi	58
Spatafore, Bryan	59
"Sunshine"	59
Zerilli, Dino	60
Baccalieri Sr, Robert "Bobby"	61
Di Palma, Thomas "Tommy"	61
Intile, Salvatore "Mustang Sally"	62
Lupo, Murf	62
Paduana, Donnie	63
Parisi, Phillip "Philly Spoons"	63
Scerbo, Guiseppe "Beppy"	64
Signore, Charles "Chucky"	64
Barese, Albert "Ally Boy"	65
Barese, Lorenzo "Larry Boy"	66
Altieri, Jimmy	67
Doria, Terry	68
Gervasi, Carlo	68
Grigio, Sammy	69
Pitsaturo, Vincent "Vinny Pitts"	69
Anastasia, Jerry	70
Curto, Raymond	70
DiMeo, Rocco	71
La Manna, Michele "Feech"	72
Malanga, " Little Pussy"	73
Martin, Romeo	73
Sasso, Cicchi	74
Cippolini, Joey	74
Anthony, Hector	75
Barone, Dick	76
Barone Sanitation	76
Caputo, Vic	77
Dupree, Warren	77
La Cerva, Adriana	78
La Manna, E Gary	79
La Manna, Jimmy	79
Massarone, "Black" Jack	79
Tiffen, Maurice	81

Teittleman, Hillel 81
Antjuan 82
Clayborn, John 83
Curtis, Credenzo 83
Johnson, Stanley 84
Ray, Rasheen 84
Special K 85
Ahmed 85
Muhammed 86
Aprile, Augustus "Little Auggie" 86
Cogo, Joseph "Joey" 87
Debbie 87
Giacalone, Angelo 88
Haydu, Barry 88
Kamal 90
Kaplan, Eli 90
Orange J 91
Reverend James Junior 91
Kolar, Emil 92
Mahaffey, Alex 92
Makazian, Vin 93
Massive Genius 93
Gia, Matush 94
Melvoin, Harold 95
Mink, Neil 95
Irish, Rusty 96
Mendez, "Yo-Yo" 96
Santiago, Reuben "The Cuban" 97
Schartz, Marty 97
Smith, Chief Doug 98
Spirodakis, Teddy 98
Tracee 99
"Juan Valdez" 99
Valery 100
Zellman, Ronald 101
Zucca, Annalisa 102
Pillsbury, Devin 103
Selgada, Blanco 103
O'Brien, Hernan 104

Eric DeBenedetto 104
Charlie Garepe 105
Leotardo, Patty... 105
Lupertazzi, Nicole 106
Millio, Gianna 106
Sacramoni, Allegra Marie 107
Sacramoni, Catherine 107
Sacramoni, Ginny 108
DeTrolio, Finn.. 109
Hauser, Don 110
Scangarelo, Hunter 110
Tannenbaum, Noah 111
Vandermeed, Ally...111
Soprano, Ercoli 112
Soprano, Harpo "Hal"... 112
Soprano, Giovanni Francis "Johnny Boy" 113
Comàre.. 114
La Paz, Valentina 114
Blundetto, Kelly 115
Blundetto, Louise.. 115
Cifaretto, Justin 115
Bonpensiero, Angie... 116
Bonpensiero, Edward "Duke" 117
Bonpensiero, Sal "Big Pussy"....................................... 118
Bonpensiero, Kevin 120
Bonpensiero, Matt 120
Dante, Gabriela 121
Dante, Heather..122
Fazio, Benny (Sr) 122
Fazio, Connie 122
Fazio, Jen 123
Gualtieri, Maria Nuccia..123
Jim, aka "Johnny Cakes" 124
Palmice, JoJo 125
Parisi, Donna 125
Pontecorvo, Ally..126
Pontecorvo, Deanna..126
Pontecorvo, Robby..127
Spatafore, Franscesca 127

Spatafore, Marie 128
Spatafore, Vito (Jr.) 129
Tom Giglione 130
Sacramoni, Johnny "Sack" 130
Rocco 131
Zucco, Victorio 131
Zucco, Mario 131
LaPenna, Jason 131
LaPenna, Richard 131
Soprano, Janice 132
Capuano, Fred 133
Isabella 133
Bones, Jimmy 133
Aprile, Jackie (Jr.) 134
Kupferberg, Eliot 134
Fazio, "Little" Benny 134
Germani, " Little" Paulie 135
Trillo, Gloria 135
Giunta, Furio 136
Skiff, Julianna 136
Parisi, Pasquale "Patsy" 137
Cifaretto, Ralph 137
Intintola, Father Phil 138
Gualtieri, Peter Paul "Walnuts" 139
Musto, Vic 139
Wegler, Robert 140
Arkaway, Aaron 140
Bucco, Art 141
Bucco, Charmaine 142
Cusamano, Jeannie 142
Cusamano, Joan 143
Fanny 144
Felstein, Fran 144
Piocosta, George 145
Sanfillipo, Roberta "Bobbi" 145
Scatino, David 146
Aprile, Rosalie 146
Baccalieri, Bobby Jr. 147
Baccalieri, Karen 148

Baccalieri, Sophia...148
Blundetto, Justin 149
Cubitoso, Frank (FBI Chief) 149
Grasso, Frank (FBI Agent)...150
Harris, Dwight (FBI Agent) 150
Lipari, Skip (FBI Agent)... 151
Marquez, Joe (FBI Agent).. 151
Sanseverino, Robyn (FBI Agent) 152
Waldrup, Deborah Ciccerone (FBI Agent) 152
April, Jackie Jr 153
List of Rats 155
List of DiMeo Family Associates.......................................156

The Sopranos Encyclopedia

Soprano, Tony

Actor: James Gandolfini

Anthony "Tony" Soprano (James Gandolfini) is the boss of the DiMeo crime family, and patriarch of the Soprano household. The series begins with an anxiety attack that motivates him to start going to therapy. His therapist, referred to him by his next door neighbor and physician, is Dr. Jennifer Melfi, a competent professional who soon finds herself struggling to negotiate the very thin line that separates her responsibilities to her patient from her wariness of getting too involved in Tony's life. Tony's immediate family consists of his daughter Meadow, his son AJ, and his wife Carmela. As the series progresses, Tony finds himself struggling to be a good father and a good mobster at the same time. He must cope with a proliferation of FBI informants and investigations. Ultimately, he is shot in the stomach by his senile Uncle Junior, and is on his way to recovery as the first part of Season Six drew to a close.

Soprano, Carmela

Actor: Edie Falco

Carmela Soprano is Tony Soprano's wife. She is principally a homemaker and wife, doing the best she can to raise her two children—Meadow and AJ—without getting them overly involved or threatened by their father's activities in the Mafia. As the series progresses, she experiences increasing distress over Tony's infidelity and life as a mobster, going so far as to separate from him briefly. This distress however, is countered with her penchant for enjoying the riches and privileges that come from being the wife of a Soprano mob boss. Throughout the series, she struggles with the cognitive dissonance she experiences as a result of disliking Tony's business while still wanting to benefit from it.

Soprano, Meadow Mariangela

Actor: Jamie-Lynn Sigler

Meadow Soprano is Tony Soprano's oldest child, currently engaged, and attending Columbia University. . Meadow is a gifted student who, like her mother, is sometimes unable to succesfully ignore her father's business, and hopes to pursue a career in law. She is currently engaged to Finn, who she met in her Sophomore year at Columbia.

Soprano, Anthony Junior, a.k.a. AJ

Actor: Robert Iler

A.J. is initially a typical adolescent, struggling with an unconfirmed diagnosis of ADHD and teenage rebellion. As the show progresses, he becomes more and more disdainful of living the life of a "whitebread wop" and gets involved with party and event planning at New York clubs.

Soprano, Livia

Actor: Nancy Marchand

Livia Soprano is mother to Tony Soprano and Soprano family matriarch who constantly finds ways to criticize Tony and his wife. She refers to her late husband as a saint, conveniently forgetting indiscretions that so angered him when he was alive. In season one, she is placed in Green Grove retirement home and is increasingly resentful of her son as a result. After cosigning and approving a hit on Tony, she dies in the second episode of season three of old age. A longer subplot had been planned for this character, but Ms. Marchand passed away. Dr. Melfi surmises that Tony's relationship with his mother may be partially responsible for his panic attacks, and governs the nature of his relationships with most women.

Anxiety Attacks

Tony Soprano, and later his son AJ, are plagued by anxiety attacks. The first show of the first season opens with Tony collapsing from an attack at his son's birthday party. His neighbor and physician refers him to Dr. Jennifer Melfi to assist him in addressing the stress that causes him to experience such acute anxiety

Animals

Animals are a consistent thematic element in the series. Tony is obsessed with a family of ducks that land in his swimming pool, tearing up when they fly away. He argues with his mistress Irina for feeding cheese doodles to ducks. He kills a mob associate because he burned down a stable-with a horse in it—to collect insurance money. Tony is manifested as a protective Rotweiler in one of Dr. Melfi's dreams. A seagull in Tony's dreams flies away with his penis. Tony's nephew sits on his girlfriend's dog by mistake and kills her, angering Tony.

Moltisanti, Christopher

Actor: Michael Imperioli

Christopher Moltisanti is second cousin to Carmela but considered a nephew and protégée of Tony's within the mob family. Christopher dreams of writing mafia movies and making it big in Hollywood, but his aspirations never come to fruition. Violent and quick tempered, he is prone to shooting first and asking questions later, though when a gun is held to his own head, he wets his pants. He occasionally dabbled in heroin till developing an addiction that landed him in rehab, and occasionally relapses in moments of extreme stress. Christopher was engaged to girlfriend Adriana, but she was killed when it was discovered she was an FBI informant. To get over her death, he marries Kelli shortly after getting her pregnant, but cheats on her while she is pregnant with Juiliana Skiff.

Rabkin, Herman "Hesh"

Actor: Jerry Adler

This non-Italian is an important part of Tony's crew who has been affiliated with the mafia since Tony's father ran the business. Hesh is perhaps the most sophisticated member of Tony's organization, as he has made money in the somewhat legitimate business of producing music in the 50s and 60s. He is a close friend to the Sopranos, and though Jewish, is regarded as trustworthy by the crew.

Pelstin, Irina

Actors: Oksana Lada and Siberia Federico (Pilot Only)

Appears in: "Pilot", "Denial, Anger, Acceptance", "Meadowlands", "College", "Pax Soprana", "A Hit is a Hit", "Guy Walks into a Psychiatrist's Office...", "Big Girls Don't Cry", "The Knight in White Satin Armor", "Fortunate Son", "Employee of the Month", "Pine Barrens", "Watching Too Much Television", "Whitecaps"

She is a Russian immigrant who acts as Tony's mistress in the first two seasons. He eventually breaks it off with her and offers $75,000 after she threatens to commit suicide. Later, he starts sleeping with her cousin, Svetlana, and to exact revenge, she informs Carmela about Tony's indiscretions.

Melfi, Jennifer, MD

Actor: Lorraine Falco

Tony's psychiatrist, who walks a narrow line in trying to help her client but not get too involved in his mafia lifestyle. She is tempted to ask for his help when she is brutally raped and her attacker is released from police custody on a technicality, but eventually decides it's best not to use his connections. While Tony occasionally gets angry with her because he's not used to people telling him things he may not want to hear, he always comes back. She is divorced with one son who is in college.

Green Grove:

Green Grove is an expensive retirement home in New Jersey where many of the mobsters place their aging mothers.

Vesuvio

Vesuvio is a restaurant owned by Tony's childhood friend Artie Bucco, along with his wife Charmaine. Tony blows it up to spare Artie the anguish of mob affiliation and subsequent loss of business early on in the series when he hears that his uncle Junior is planning to execute a ht there. Eventually Artie and Charmaine start a new restaurant called Nuovo Vesuvio.

Triborough Towers Garbage

Triborough Towers Garage is a company vying to take some of the Soprano crew's business. They backed off on their bid when the heir to the company, Emile Kolar, was shot in the head, and they presumed him missing.

Father Phil

Father Phil is a Catholic priest who often has questionable motives in dealing with female members of his congregation, and has nearly succumbed to temptation with Carmela in the past.

Stugots

Stugots is the name of Tony's boat.

Aprile, Giacomo "Jackie Sr"

Actor: Michael Rispoli

Can be found in episodes: "46 Long", "Denial, Anger, Acceptance", "Meadowlands", "...To Save Us All From Satan's Power"

Giacomo Aprile is a late acting boss of the crew, who died of cancer without naming a successor. He leaves behind his wife, Rosalie, and his son, Jackie Jr.

Filone, Brendan:

Actor: Anthony DeSando

Appears in: "46 Long", "Denial, Anger, Acceptance", "Meadowlands", "The Legend of Tennessee Moltisanti"

Friend of Christopher's who hijacks the trucks that Junior is being paid to protect. Ultimately, Junior decides he is a loose cannon and has Mike Palmice shoot him while he's in the bathtub. Christopher is devastated and Tony staples Mike

Palmice's suit to his body in retaliation on Christopher's behalf. Later, when Christopher shoots Palmice on Tony's orders, he gets his revenge, saying "my friend Brendan, you shot him in his bathtub naked, no way to run."

Comley Trucks

Chris and Brendan Filone hijack DVD players from a Comley Truck and later are in trouble for it, as Junior had been paid to protect the vehicles.

Satriale's

Satriale's is a pork store where the crew hangs out. The mob was able to take it over because the former owner couldn't pay gambling debts. In Tony's childhood, he had his first anxiety attack because he saw his father cut a man's finger off in Satriale's.

Bada Bing

Bada-Bing is a strip club owned by Silvio Dante where the crew hangs out, enjoys the girls, and talks business.

Teittleman, Shlomo

Actor: Chuck Low
Can be found in episodes: "Denial, Anger, Acceptance"
A practicing Hassidic Jew and co-owner of the Flyaway Motel. In 1999 Teitlemann hired the Soprano crew intimidate his son in law, Ariel, to agree to a divorce from Teitlemann's daughter without the 50% cut of the business he was asking for. Teitlemann eventually negotiated with Ariel himself, and tried to pay Sopranos off with a wad of cash instead of the promised share in the business - Tony refused this and insisted on his promised 25%. Teitlemann had no choice to capitulate. He was left owning 40% of his business, and knowing he was partners with the mob.

Ariel

Actor: Ned Eisenberg

Can be found in episodes: "Denial, Anger, Acceptance"

Ariel is a son in law to Shlomo Teitleman. Tony and his crew are charged with intimidating him into walking away from the hotel upon the divorce of his wife with a smaller sum of money than he had originally wished. He doesn't fear death, so he doesn't give in until Tony and his crew threaten to castrate him.

Masada

Masada is the site of a long siege between a small number of Jew and legions of Roman soldiers. The siege ended in the mass suicide of the Jews who preferred death to enslavement. Ariel tells this story when threatened with death.

Golem

Teitlemann calls Tony this name. Golem a Yiddish word with a few possible meanings. It can refer to anything that is incomplete or in an embryonic stage, or an entity made from inanimate matter, it can mean monster, or it can simply mean "fool".

Piocosta, Jeremy

Actor: Teddy Colluca

Appears in: "Meadowlands"

Jeremy Picosta is a classmate of AJ's who backs down from a schoolyard fight because he fears AJ's father.

Meadowlands

Meadowlands is a spot in New Jersey that is notorious for being a dumping ground for the victims of Mafia violence

Petrulio, Fabian "Febby"

Actor: Tony Ray Rossi

Can be found in episodes: "College"

Petrulio was a member of DiMeo crime family who ratted them out to the FBI and was then placed in the witness protection program. He is killed after Tony sees him at a gas station in Maine while taking his daughter to look at colleges.

Hawthorne, Nathanial

Tony is unnerved by a quote of his that says: "No man... can wear one face to himself and another to the multitude, without finally getting bewildered as to which one may be true."

Lupertazzi Crime Family

The Lupertazzi crime family is a New York Crime family headed by Carmine Lupertazzi and then Johnny Sack.

Down Neck

Down Neck is a section of Newark where Tony and his family live and his father did business.

Cusamano, Bruce, MD

Acto: Robert Lupone

Appears in: "A Hit is a Hit", "Isabella", "Funhouse", "Whitecaps"

Tony's next door nieghbor, a "white bread wop", who refers him to Dr. Melfi.

Santini, Richard:

Actor: Nick Fowler

Appears in: "A Hit is a Hit"

Richard Santini is a childhood friend of Adriana and lead singer of the band Visiting Day. He currently lives at home because he is recovering from an injury he sustained when trying to grill a trout with a downed power line.

Visiting Day

Band fronted by Adriana's childhood friend Richie Santini. She tries to produce a hit record for the band with Christopher's financing. However, Chris ultimately decides that the band is not that good and stops supporting the project.

La Cerva, Liz

Actor: Patty McCormack

Appears in: "Full Leather Jacket", "Watching Too Much Television", "Long Term Parking", "The Ride", "Kaisha"

Liz La Cerva is a sister of the late Jackie Aprile, Sr. and Richie Aprile, mother to Adriana La Cerva, and sister-in-law to Rosalie Aprile Liz was against Adriana's relationship with Christopher due to his heroin habit and penchant for physically abusing her. After Adriana was killed in 2004, Liz, who thought that she had just disappeared, informed by the FBI her that her daughter was believed to be dead and that they suspected Chris Moltisani. She later attempted suicide.

Safir, Amy

Actor: Alicia Witt

Appears in: "D-Girl"
Amy Safir is the fiancee of Christopher Moltisanti's cousin Gregory Moltisanti. She had a brief affair with Christopher when he was trying to get his script turned into a movie.

Francesco, Tina

Actor: Vanessa Ferlito

Appears in: "Another Toothpick" and "Rat Pack"

Tina was the girlfriend of Soprano family associate Salvatore "Mustang Sally" Intile before his death. Tina was also friends with Adriana, but upset Adriana by constantly flirting with her fiance, Christopher..

Testa, Matt

Actor: Cameron Boyd

Appears in: "Everybody Hurts", "All Happy Families...", "All Due Respect", "Johnny Cakes"

Matt is a friend of AJ Soprano's who later works with AJ at Blockbuster.

Dolan, JT

Actor: Tim Daly

Appears in: "In Camelot", "Mayham"

JT Dolan is a screenwriter and friend asscoicate of Christopher's from rehab. JT borrows money to gamble and fails to pay it back on time. Eventually, Chris has JT abducted from a writing class he teaches by Murmur and Benny Fazio, and offers to forgive the debt if JT writes a screenplay for his movie project.

Massarone Construction

Massarone Construction was subjected to protests for failing to hire enough minorities, and asked the Soprano crew to bring them to a halt. Tony splits the money paid to end the protests with the protest leader, Reverend Herman James. Reverend James states that his deceased father would not have liked the arrangement, but that it is a business arrangement that could not be refused.

"You Bark, I Bite"

Christopher's unfinished screenplay about mob life.

Ramsey Sports and Outdoors

Ramsey Sports and Outdoors is a former Scatino family business now owned by Tony due to high losses incurred by Davey Scatino at a high stakes poker game.

Kirilenko, Svetlana

Actor: Alla Kliouka Schaffer

Appears in: "The Knight in White Satin Armor", "Proshai, Livushka", "Fortunate Son", "Whoever Did This", "The Strong, Silent Type", "Calling All Cars", "Whitecaps"

Svetlana is the cousin of Tony's ex-comàre Irina and runs a visiting nurse association, and is missing a leg due to a childhood infection that led to its amputation. She was first hired as Livia Soprano's nurse, and becomes embroiled in conflict with a Soprano when Janice asks the whereabouts of Livia's records and learns that they had been promised to Svetlana. In revenge, Janice steals Svetlana's prosthetic leg, and Svetlana sics Russian mob on Janice. She eventually produces the leg. Svetlana resurfaces as Uncle Junior's nurse after he suffers a fall at the courthouse, and Tony has sex with Svetlana but soon comes to regret it when Irina tells Carmela about the affair.

Baccalieri, Dominica

Actor: Kimberly Laughlin and Brianna Laughlin

Can be found in episodes: "Members Only", "Join the Club" , "The Ride", "Kaisha"

Domenica the daughter of Bobby Baccalieri and Janice Soprano, born sometime between 2004 and 2006.

Cammarata, Brian

Actor: Matthew Del Negro

Can be found in episodes: "The Weight", "Pie-O-My", "Everybody Hurts", "Watching Too Much Television", "Mergers and Acquisitions", "Eloise", "Whitecaps", "Marco Polo"

Brian is Carmela's cousin and a financial advisor, and helped her plan for the unthinkable should Tony be hurt, killed, or incarcerated.

Blundetto, Quintina Pollio

Actor: Barbara Andres and Rae Allen

Can be found in episodes: "Funhouse", "Proshai, Livushka", "Rat Pack", "Irregular Around the Margins", "Marco Polo", "The Test Dream"

Quintina is Livia's younger sister, and Tony B's mother.

Blundetto, Tony

Actor: David Buscemi

Tony Blundetto was the father of three children - two sons, Justin and Jason (conceived by having his semen smuggled out of prison) -- and an estranged daughter, Kelly. Blundetto and Tony Soprano were close childhood friends and both looked to the mob for future careers. Blundetto was moving up the ranks of the mafia until the mid 1980s when he was arrested for attempted hijacking. He was then incarcerated for 17 years, which gave him plenty of time to get to know Angelo Garape of the Lupertazzi crime family. Tony and Angelo were released from jail at around the same time as colleagues Phil Leotardo and Feech La Manna, earning the nickname "the class of 2004."

After he was released on parole, "Tony B" initially decided to turn away from a life of crime and pursued a career as a licensed massage therapist. However, Blundetto gradually became more and more frustrated with the struggles of working for a living, and eventually turned back to the mob for his income.

With his strong feelings of entitlement and thirst for quick money, Blundetoo joined Little Carmine in the war with Johnny Sack and didn't get the go-ahead from his cousin Tony Soprano first. This involved a contract by Angelo Garepe to kill Leotardo crew associate Joe Peeps, a mission that Tony B. execucutive successfully, killing Peeps' female companion, and getting his foot run over by a car in the process.

Word traveled fast that Tony B had been involved in the killings, and Tony Soprano covered for Blundetto and tried to convince Johnny Sack that his cousin wasn't the perp who shot Peeps and his cumare.

Tony had no success, however, and Phil Leotardo and his brother Billy killed Angelo to avenge Joey, and Tony B in turn hunted down the Leotardo brothers to avenge Angelo's death and killed Billy, which in turn caused Phil want to kill Tony B for vengeance for Billy's death. Tony Soprano eventually realized that he couldn't cover for his cousin forever. He killed Blundetto personally in lieu of Phil's vengeance so he would have a painless death.

Despite being dead, Tony B managed to appear in season 6 in a coma-induced dream of Tony's, trying to beckon him into a house, but he is only credited as "Man", not Tony Blundetto.

De Angelis, Hugh

Actor: Tom Aldredge

Can be found in episodes: "Guy Walks into a Psychiatrist's Office...", "Full Leather Jacket", "Funhouse", "Proshai, Livushka", "Fortunate Son", "Another Toothpick", "University", "Second Opinion", "He is Risen", "The Telltale Moozadell", "Pine Barrens", "For All Debts Public and Private", "The Strong, Silent Type", "Calling All Cars", "Whitecaps", "Sentimental Education", "Marco Polo", "All Due Respect", "Members Only", "Mayham", "Live Free or Die", "Kaisha"

Hugh De Angelis is Carmela's father, a retired contractor, who is in his mid 70s. Hugh has been married to his wife Mary for over 40 years and is a resident of West Orange, New Jersey. Although presumably now retired, Hugh had worked as a contractor, including building Tony and Carmela's house.

Hugh also has a brother, Lester. Hugh is very traditional, even taking Tony's side at times when Tony and Carmela were separated, expressing reluctance to go to a family gathering when "the man of the house" was not there. Eventually, Carmela and Hugh feud over this and other transgressions, but Carmela reconcile enough for him to attend Christmas celebrations at the Soprano home.

De Angelis, Mary Pellegrino

Actor: Suzanne Shepherd

Can be found in episodes: "Guy Walks Into A Psychiatrist's Office...", "Full Leather Jacket", "Funhouse", "Proshai, Livushka", "Fortunate Son", "Another Toothpick", "University", "Second Opinion", "He is Risen", "The Telltale Moozadell", "Pine Barrens", "For All Debts Public and Private", "The Strong, Silent Type", "Calling All Cars", "Whitecaps", "Marco Polo", "Mayham", "Live Free or Die", "Luxury Lounge", "Kaisha"

Mary De Angelis is Carmela's mother. She is in her mid 70s, married to her husband Hugh De Angelis of over 40 years. Mary was initially very against her daughter's marriage to Tony, which did not improve when Livia told Carmela that "Tony would get bored of her." Mary had a brother named Febby who died of cancer. Mary and Carmela have occasionally been at odds with eachother since Mary remains uncomfortable with having Tony around her "cultured Italian friends".

Giglione, Tom

Actor: Ed Vassalo

Can be found in episodes: "Guy Walks into a Psychiatrist's Office...", "The Happy Wanderer", "Funhouse", "Proshai, Livushka", "Where's Johnny?", "In Camelot", "Mayham", "Moe N' Joe"

Tom Giglione is Barbara's husband and Tony and Janice's brother-in-law. He and Barbara live in Brewster, New York with their two children.

Giglione, Barbara Soprano

Actor: Nicole Burdette, Danielle Di Vecchio

Can be found in episodes: "Guy Walks into a Psychiatrist's Office...", "The Happy Wanderer", "Funhouse", "Proshai, Livushka", "Where's Johnny?", "In Camelot", "Members Only", "Join the Club", "Mayham", "Moe N' Joe"

Barbara is Tony's younger sister who lives in Brewster, New York. She is the mother of two children and is actively involved in helping to care for Junior in his old age.

After Tony's shooting, Barbara, who previously had not been around much, took part in keeping a round-the-clock vigil for

Tony at the hospital and later attended family Sunday dinners at his home.

Moltisani, Joanne

Actor: Nancy Cassaro (2000) and Marianne Leone (2002-present)

Can be found in episodes: "From Where To Eternity", "For All Debts Public and Private", "Watching Too Much Television", "The Strong, Silent Type", "Rat Pack", "Marco Polo", "All Due Respect"

Joanne is the widow of Richard "Dickie" Moltisanti and the mother of Christopher Moltisanti. Joanne has battled alcoholism for many years, and is a devoted mother. She kept a vigil at her son's bedside when he was shot in 2000, and when her nephew Tony Blundetto killed Billy Leotardo, Christopher hid from Phil Leotardo at her home. Despite being intimidated, she refused to give up her son.

DiMeo, Domenico Ercoli "Eckley"

Actor: Unseen character

Referenced in: "Meadowlands", "Pax Soprana", "Rat Pack"

The founder of the DiMeo Crime Family, Domenico Ercoli DiMeo, AKA 'Old Man' AKA 'Eckley' DiMeo, is the official crime boss of the Soprano/DiMeo family. Though a force to be reckoned with in the 1950s, he is currently serving a life sentence in a high security prison, where he has been since 1997.

Palmice, Mikey "Grab Bag"

Actor: Al Sapienza

Can be found in episodes: "46 Long", "Denial, Anger, Acceptance", "Meadowlands", "Pax Soprana", "The Legend of Tennessee Moltisanti", "Boca", "Nobody Knows Anything", "Isabella", "I Dream of Jeannie Cusamano", "The Test Dream"

Mikey Palmice was Corrado "Junior" Soprano's chauffeur and strongman, working alongside Chucky Signore, instrumental in helping arrange the attempt on Tony's life in Season I. This failed attempt led Tony to get Chucky and Mikey. Chris was only too happy to take on the job. When hunted down, Mikey tried to blame the assasination attempt, and death of Chris' friend Brendan on Chris, however, did not believe him. "My friend

Brendan, you shot him in his bathtub naked, no way to run." Tony was executed and left in the woods.

Mikey is survived by his wife JoJo and two sons, Francis Albert and Michael, Jr.

Joseph "Beppy" Sasso

Can be found in episodes: "I Dream of Jeannie Cusamano"

Acted as underboss to Junior Soprano until his arrest in 1999.

Soprano, Corrano John "Junior"

Actor: Dominic Chianese

Junior is Tony Soprano's father's brother. Junior always watched after Tony, but after his father Johnny Boy's death from emphysema, Junior became Tony's surrogate father. He eventually, however, came to resent Tony because of his quick ascendance in the DiMeo crime family.

Upon the death of Jackie Aprile, Tony and Junior fought for control of the family and eventually reached a compromise. Although Junior technically became the boss, Tony really ran the show, using Junior as a front to distract law enforcement. Tensions still remained high and when Junior heard from Livia that Tony saw a therapist, this was the straw and he ordered a hit on Tony.

The hit was foiled and Tony arranged for Junior's top trigger men, Mikey Palmice and Chucky Signore, to be assassinated. At the same time, Junior was arrested on federal racketeering charges, and the arrest of his underboss, Beppy Sasso, followed shortly therafter. Junior, however, found various ways to get around his house arrest - using his doctor's office to conduct business (until the feds placed an agent there posing as a nurse) and attending as many funerals and family functions as possible.

Junior's replacement capo, Philly "Spoons" Parisi, couldn't keep his mouth shut about Junior and Livia's plan to whack Tony, so Tony had him killed, and then moved two soldiers from Junior's crew, Patsy Parisi and Gigi Cestone, over to his crew. This left Junior with Murf Lupo as capo and Beppy Scerbo and Bobby Baccalieri AKA Bobby Bacala, as soldiers. Through Bobby, Tony informed Junior that while he could keep the title of Boss, Tony would only let him keep a 5% tribute, which would be (barely) enough to live on.

Soon thereafter, captain Richie Aprile was released from prison, and actively sought Junior's friendship. Junior found himself in the middle of an escalating power struggle between Richie and Tony. Junior was extremely conflicted over which side to favor, but eventually decided to tell Tony of Richie's plans against him. Grateful for the warning, Tony doubled Junior's percentage of his former businesses, and the two made amends

Although Junior has survived cancer and prison, 'mini-strokes' and the confinement of house arrest has since left him confused, depressed, and increasingly dependent on family care and support.

In season six of The Sopranos, Junior's dementia has worsened, and he suffers from paranoid delusions that his dead enemy "Little Pussy" Malanga is after him. Tony arrives at Junior's house one evening and finds that his uncle is missing his false teeth, and sends him upstairs to retrieve them while he prepares dinner. When Junior hears Tony's voice from downstairs telling him that dinner is ready, Junior descends the stairs and, believing his nephew to be Malanga, shoots Tony in the abdomen. He then runs and hides in the bedroom closet while Tony manages to dial 911 before losing consciousness.

Junior remains confused and distressed by the proceedings that followed and denies that he could have deliberately attacked his own nephew.

Alfie

Actor: Michael Goduti

Can be found in episodes: "Eloise"

Alfie participates in vandalizing the restaurant over the HUD dispute.

Annunziata, Perry

Actor: Louis Gross

Can be found in episodes: "Mr. & Mrs. John Sacrimoni Request", "Live Free or Die", "The Ride" and "Cold Stones"

Perry Annunziata served as a bodyguard and driver for Tony Soprano while Tony recovered from the wound he sustained when his uncle shot him in the stomach. Tony picked a fight with Perry at Satriale's to demonstrate that despite having been shot, he was still in robust health, picking on Perry specifically because of his muscular build. Tony later paid Perry off as an apology and Perry in turn resumed his duties by accompanying Tony to the Feast of St. Elzear and Christopher Moltisanti's bachelor party.

Bevilaqua, Mathew

Actor: Lillo Brancato Jr.

Can be found in episodes: "Guy Walks into a Psychiatrist's Office...", "Do Not Resuscitate", "The Happy Wanderer", "Full Leather Jacket", "From Where to Eternity", "Bust Out"

Matthew Bevilaqua was Sean Gismonte's partner-in-crime and an associate in the Tony Soprano crew. He hoped to ascend in the ranks of the crime family, participating in a stock scam with

Christopher, but getting in trouble for stealing cars without permission.

In hopes of gaining recognition from Richie Aprile, who disliked Chris for his physical abuse of his niece Adriana, Matt and Sean tried to execute a drive by. This, however, didn't go as planned and Chris shot Sean to death and Chris was wounded. Matt went to Richie for help but Richie refused, and Matt went into hiding. Eventually, Pussy found him, and he and Tony beat and murdered him. Unbenknownst to them, there was a witness, however, the witness backed down when he realized that it was Tony Soprano that he'd fingered.

Blundetto, Pat

Actor: Frank Albanese

Can be found in episodes: "Cold Cuts" and "Long Term Parking"

Pat Blundetto is the uncle of Tony Soprano and Tony Blundetto. He owns a farm that hosts an informal graveyard of several bodies that have been hidden there over the years.

Caporale, Corky

Actor: Edoardo Ballerini

Can be found in episodes: "Live Free or Die", "Luxury Lounge", "The Ride"

An associate of Christopher Moltisanti, a speaker of Italian, and a heroin addict. He was enlisted to accomodate the Italian hitmen who were to execute a hit on Rusty Millio.. Christopher paid him for the job with heroin and in turn, Corky delivered weapons and instructions at a remote spot, and the hit went smoothly. Chris, when delivering the second installment of heroin in exchange for the job, was tempted to shoot up, and relapsed into addiction.

Cortese, Frankie

Actor: Tony Siragusa

Can be found in episodes: "Irregular Around the Margins", "Marco Polo", "Unidentified Black Males" and "Long Term Parking"

Frankie Cortese served as a driver and bodyguard for Tony as an associate of the Soprano crime family in 2004.

De La Rosa, Peter "Petey"

Actor: Jeffrey M Marchetti

Can be found in episodes: "Eloise", "Whitecaps", "Two Tonys", "In Camelot", "Unidentified Black Males", "Mr. & Mrs. John Sacrimoni Request", "Moe N' Joe"

Petey is primarily noteworthy for killing Stanley Johnson and Credenzo Curtis with Benny Fazio, on orders from Christopher Moltisanti, and his role at Satriale's as a doorman.

DiBartolo, Cary

Actor: James Vincent Romano

Referenced in: "Mayham", "The Fleshy Part of the Thigh"

An associate of Paulie Walnuts who accompanied him on a robbery of Columbian drug dealers in 2006, and threatened an EMT who had allegedly taken Tony's money when he was in the hospital.

Giarizzo, Gaetano

Actor: Stelio Savante

Can be found in episodes: "Full Leather Jacket"

An Italian associate of Furio Guante. Most noteworthy for going with Furio to Sean and Matt's apartment to collect money for Tony Soprano.

Gervasi, Burt

Actor: Artie Pasquale

Can be found in episodes: "In Camelot", "Luxury Lounge", "The Ride"

A cousin to Carlo Gervasi, Burt was made a formal member of the Soprano crime family in 2006, at the same time as Phil Leotardo's soldier Gerry Torciano.

Gismonte, Sean

Actor: Chris Tardio

Can be found in episodes: "Guy Walks into a Psychiatrist's Office...", "Do Not Resuscitate", "The Happy Wanderer", "Full Leather Jacket"

Sean Gismonte was Matthew Bevilaqua's partner in crime and an associate in the Gualtieri crew in 2000, who, like Matthew, hoped to ascend in the ranks of the DiMeo crime family. In addition to his involvment in a stock scam and a series of car thefts, he and Christopher and Matt broke several bank safes.

After these low level jobs that required high-level tributes, he and Sean determined that the best boost for their careers would be to whack Chris, a made man, in order to get recognized by Richie Aprile, who they knew resented Chris for physically abusing his niece, Adriana.

To further this goal, Matt and Sean planned a drive-by hit as Chris left the Skyways Dinner in Kearny, however, Sean was shot and killed.

Georgie

Actor: Frank Santorelli

Can be found in episodes: "46 Long", "Pax Soprana", "The Legend of Tennessee Moltisanti", "University", "Second Opinion", "For All Debts Public and Private", "Christopher", "Watching Too Much Television", "The Strong, Silent Type", "Where's Johnny", "In Camelot", "Cold Cuts"

Georgie was a bartender at the Bada Bing who was occasionally involved in peripheral illegal activities with the DiMeo crime family.

He is most noteworthy for setting off Tony's short fuse with his slowness and getting beat up several times as a result. He also received a serious injury when Ralphie smacked Georgie in the eye with a lock and chain while imitating the movie, "Gladiator", and when he suffered hearing damage from a brutal beating at the hands of Tony Soprano. This was the straw that led him to leave the Bing and Tony, who felt guilty, gave money to Paulie to give to Georgie to make sure his medical ailments would be treated properly.

Ianucci, Corky

Actor: Unseen character

Referenced in: "Whoever Did This"

Corky is a Soprano associate whose primary skill is setting fires that appear accidental. He is best known for burning down the Vesuvio and possibly for setting fire to the stables that killed Pie-O-My.

Moltisanti, Richard "Dickie"

Actor: Unseen character

Referenced in: "From Where to Eternity", "For All Debts Public and Private"

Former soldier in the Soprano crew and Christopher's father. He is remembered as a stand-up guy who remained stand-up so long as you were on his good side. Dickie was killed during Christopher's infancy, right outside the house while bringing TV trays home. Lt. Barry Haydu investigated his murder but found no leads, however, in 2002, Christopher learned from Tony that Haydu himself was the culprit. Christopher murdered Haydu in his home as a result.

Zancone, James "Murmur"

Actor: Lenny Venito

Can be found in episodes: "Members Only", "Mayham", "Mr. & Mrs. John Sacrimoni Request", "Live Free or Die", "Luxury Lounge", "The Ride", "Cold Stones", "Kaisha"

A friend to Christopher as well as his AA sponsor, Murmur is also extremely adept at forging documents. He is noteworthy for his involvement in the kidnapping of J.T. Dolan alongside Benny Fazio, his participation in a credit card scam, and his trip to Hollywood with Christopher where he and Chris robbed Lauren Bacall of a gift basket she got for attending an awards ceremony.

Cestone, Gigi

Actor: John Fiore

Can be found in episodes: "Guy Walks into a Psychiatrist's Office...", "Do Not Resuscitate", "Big Girls Don't Cry", "Funhouse", "Mr. Ruggerio's Neighborhood", "Proshai, Livushka", "Fortunate Son", "Employee of the Month", "Another Toothpick", "University", "He Is Risen", "...To Save Us All From Satan's Power" and "The Test Dream"

Formerly a member of Junior's crew he turned to soldiering for Tony after Philly Parisi was executed. defected to Tony

Soprano's crew in 1999 after shot and killed Philly Parisi (the acting capo of Junior's crew while Junior was incarcerated) on Tony's orders. The hit was in order because Philly had spread rumors about Tony and Junior's beef.

Gigi became Capo after Richie Aprile disappeared, and as capo, ordered Bobby Bacala to whack Mustang Sally.

He met his maker while on the toilet, dying from a combination of heart trouble, stress, and constipation.

Cippolina, "Big" Frank

Actor: Michael Squicciarini

Can be found in episodes: "Toodle Fucking-Oo", "Bust Out"

Most notable for an argument with Paulie Walnuts at the Bing.

Gaeta, Peter "Beansie"

Actor: Paul Herman

Can be found in episodes: "Toodle Fucking-Oo", "Full Leather Jacket" "Bust Out", "Calling All Cars"

Peter "Beansie" Gaeta is most noteworthy for trying to dodge paying Richie money owed after he got out of prison. After Beansie refused to attend Richie's party, and then offered Richie bribe him with a free veal parmesan sandwich, but refused to cough up the dough, Richie first broke a hot pot of coffee over Beansie's head, then beat him up, then finally ran him over with his car and turned Beansie into a paraplegic.

Greco, Dante

Actor: Anthony J Ribustello

Can be found in episodes: "Irregular Around the Margins", "All Due Respect", "Members Only", "Mr. & Mrs. John Sacrimoni Request" and "Live Free or Die"

Member of the Aprile crew often peripherally involved in discussions and various illegal activities.

Coniglio, Bobby

Actor: Vito Antuofermo

Can be found in episodes: "House Arrest", "Proshai, Livushka",

Also known as Bobby Zanone. Bobby was a member of Richie Aprile's crew.

The character is played by Vito Antuofermo, the former undisputed Middleweight Boxing Champion of the world (1979-1980).

DiGioia, Corky

Actor: Duke Valenti

Can be found in episodes: "Irregular Around the Margins", Biker and associate of the Soprano family.

Dogsy

Actor: Kevin Interdonato

Can be found in episodes: "Calling All Cars", "Eloise", "Whitecaps"

An associate in the Aprile crew who put the screws to the HUD appraiser.

Donny K

Actor: Raymond Franza

Can be found in episodes: "Full Leather Jacket", "Proshai, Livushka", "He Is Risen", "No Show" and "The Weight"

Member of the Aprile crew, most noteworthy for being beaten and peed on by Johnny Sack following Ralphie's insult of Ginny Sack. Donny suffered nerve damage from the incident and has not been seen since.

Molinaro, Jason

Actor: William DiMeo

Can be found in episodes: "Irregular Around the Margins", "Unidentified Black Males", "All Due Respect", "Mayham", "Mr. & Mrs. John Sacrimoni Request" and "The Ride"

Member of the Aprile crew. Responsible for organising Joe "Peeps" Peparelli's headstone following his death - failed to have it correctly spelled, the final product being simply "Joe Peeps." Accompanied Vito when passing on information about the Columbian drug money heist in 2006. Stood guard outside the

ICU as Tony recovered from his gutshot. Later took part in a card game at Satriale's that took place as T rejoined the crew. Jason helped to break up an altercation between Paulie Gaultieri and Bobby Baccala at the Feast of St. Elzear festival.

Carlo Renzi

Actor: Louis Crugnali

Can be found in episodes: "The Telltale Moozadell" and "Amour Fou"

Jackie Aprile Jr. and Dino Zerilli's friend, and participant in the attempted robbery of Eugene Pontecorvo's Saturday night card game. Carlo was recruited because he owned a large shotgun. Unfortunately, he was not quick enough on the draw with it, as he was killed during the robbery by Christopher Moltisanti.

Spatafore, Bryan

Actor: Vincent J Orofino

Can be found in episodes: "Full Leather Jacket", "Another Toothpick", "Cold Stones"

Brother of Vito Spatafore, and partner in Spatafore Bros Construction. Among the most noteworthy of Bryan's activities include a beating he recieved by Mustang Sally.
As a result, he was expected to remain a "vegetable" for life. Bryan, however, against all odds made a partial recovery and attended a family dinner. As he remained silent throughout, it is unknown if Bryan has suffered major or minor brain damage from the assault.

"Sunshine"

Actor: Paul Mazursky

Can be found in episodes: "The Happy Wanderer", "Amour Fou"

Sunshine was a card dealer who was was killed in 2001 when Jackie Aprile, Jr. and his friends tried to rob the Saturday night game.

Zerilli, Dino

Actor: Andrew Davoli

Can be found in episodes: "Fortunate Son", "He Is Risen", "The Telltale Moozadell", "……To Save Us All From Satan's Power", "Amour Fou"

Dino was Jackie Aprile, Jr.'s friend and partner in crime in a card game robbery in order to impress the higher mob associates and ascend the ranks quickly. Things do not go their way when Sunshine gets shot during the robbery, leaving Carlo dead and Furio wounded. Dino and Jackie Jr. try to get away, but their driver had hit the road as soon as he'd heard the gunshots. Dino Zerilli was shot in the face and killed as a result.

Baccalieri Sr, Robert "Bobby"

Actor: Burt Young

Can be found in episodes: "Another Toothpick"

Father of Bobby "Bacala" Bacalieri and soldier in Junior Soprano's crew in his younger days. Returned to New Jersey from semi-retirement in 2001. Despite his age and infirmity from a battle with lung cancer, Tony Soprano gave him the task of killing his godson, Salvatore "Mustang Sally" Intile in retribution for the unprovoked beating of Bryan Spatafore. Though he successfully carried out the hit, he died after losing control of his car and crashing into a telegraph pole on his way home.

Di Palma, Thomas "Tommy"

Actor: Ed Setrakian

Can be found in episodes: "Where's Johnny"

Tommy is an elderly soldier in Junior Soprano's crew who is responsible for looking after him as his dementia gets wors.

Intile, Salvatore "Mustang Sally"

Actor: Brian Tarantina

Can be found in episodes: "Another Toothpick"

Godson of Robert Bacalieri, Sr., who dated Adriana's friend Tiny. Mustang Sally and Tina had a heated argument in the street, prompting Tina to ask a passerby-who happened to be Bryan Spatafore oof Spatafore Bros construction - Mustang Sally beat him into a coma with a golf club. Bryan Spatafore's brother, Vito Spatafore, was a made man and demanded vengeance, so Tony dispatched Bobby Baccaliere to kill him. The hit went smoothly but Baccalieri died in a car crash on the way home.

Lupo, Murf

Actor: Val Bisoglio

Can be found in episodes: "For All Debts Public and Private", "Christopher", and "Pie-o-my."

Elderly soldier and former capo of Junior Soprano's crew, replacing Philly Parisi, and later replaced by Bobby Bacala.

Paduana, Donnie

Actor: David Wike

Can be found in episodes: "Isabella"

Associate of Junior's Crew who was asked to provide hired guns to take out Tony Soprano. Padua, however, made a joke about Livia ordering the hit, which led Junior to conclude he had a big mouth, which in turn led Mikey Palmice to shoot him in the side of the head and leave him dead behind the wheel of his car.

Parisi, Phillip "Philly Spoons"

Actor: Dan Grimaldi

Can be found in episodes: "Guy Walks into a Psychiatrist's Office..." and "Funhouse"

Identical twin brother of Patsy Parisi, whacked for spreading that Tony had tried to smother Livia Soprano. After his death, he made an appearance in Tony's dream while he was suffering from food .

Scerbo, Guiseppe "Beppy"

Actor: Joe Pucillo

Can be found in episodes: "Pilot", "I Dream of Jeannie Cusamano", "...To Save Us All From Satan's Power", "Calling All Cars", "Eloise" and "Whitecaps"

Beppy is an elderly soldier in the Junior Soprano crew who can be counted on to stand by Junior.

Signore, Charles "Chucky"

Actor: Sal Ruffino

Can be found in episodes: "Nobody Knows Anything", "Isabella", "I Dream of Jeannie Cusamano"

Mikey Palmice's partner and another of Uncle Junior's cronies, killed personally by Tony Soprano at the marina to prevent any more attempts on his life.

Barese, Albert "Ally Boy"

Actor: Richard Maldone

Can be found in episodes: "The Knight in White Satin Armor", "Proshai, Livushka", "Fortunate Son", "Amour Fou", "For All Debts Public and Private", "No Show" "The Weight", "Watching Too Much Television", "The Strong, Silent Type", "Rat Pack"

Cousin of Lawrence "Larry Boy" Barese and acting capo of the Barese crew when Larry Boy was in jail.

When Richie Aprile wanted to make a move against Tony Soprano, he approached Albert, but Albert demurred. Albert was also involved in a "garbage war" with Ralph Cifaretto that Tony feared would bring police attention on his crew. Tony settled the dispute between the two at a in his backyard.

Also noteworthy is that it was also at Albert's birthday party that the infamous "weight" remark was said by Ralphie about Ginny Sack.

Barese, Lorenzo "Larry Boy"

Actor: Tony Darrow

Can be found in episodes: "Meadowlands", "Pax Soprana", "The Legend of Tennessee Moltisanti", "Boca", "I Dream of Jeannie Cusamano", "Christopher", "Pie-O-My", "Calling All Cars", "Whitecaps", "All Due Respect", "Join the Club", "Mayham", "The Ride"

Capo of the Barese crew; Godfather of Benny Fazio cousin of Albert Barese. A trusted associate, Larry Boy moved his mother to the Green Grove retirement community so that he could conduct surreptitious meetings with Tony.

Larry Boy was also arrested at around the same time a Junior, and was a second defendant in the courtroom during Junior's RICO trial. Three years after the indictments Larry Boy was released following a mistrial and put under house arrest, where he still managed to take back his crew from Ally Boy.

Altieri, Jimmy

Actor: Joe Badalucco

Can be found in episodes: "Boca", "Nobody Knows Anything", "Isabella", "I Dream of Jeannie Cusamano", "...To Save Us All From Satan's Power"

Former capo in the DiMeo/Soprano crime family, Jimmy was arrested when the FBI found him in a room filled with pool tables that hid guns. Rumore has it that he "flipped" at this time.

Tony grew suspicious of Jimmy shortly after he was busted due to his early release from custody, his constant questions about mob activities, and odd behavior. As such, acting on orders Christopher lured Jimmy to a hotel room with the promise of "Russian broads" and Silvio shot him in the back of his head. Jimmy's body was found in an alley with a rat stuffed in his mouth.

Doria, Terry

Actor: Ron Castellano

Can be found in episodes: "Cold Cuts", "Live Free or Die", "Cold Stones"

Member of Carlo Gervasi's crew who most notably helped locate hidden Vespas that Johnny Sack kept hidden from Tony.

Gervasi, Carlo

Actor: Arthur J. Nascarella

Can be found in episodes: "For All Debts Public and Private", "No Show", "Christopher", "Pie-O-My", "The Strong, Silent Type", "Two Tonys", "Sentimental Education", "In Camelot", "Unidentified Black Males", "Cold Cuts", "Long Term Parking", "All Due Respect", "Members Only", "Join the Club", "Live Free or Die", "The Ride", "Moe N' Joe", "Cold Stones", "Kaisha"

The captain of Jimmy Altieri's old crew, most notable for operating the Bloomfield Ave casino, and assisting in port hijackings.

Gervasi was given all of Vito Spatafore's construction business in addition to the ports. Gervasi was also outspoken about his disapproval of Spatafore's homosexuality. In addition, Gervasi disposed of Gamiello's body and putting the head in a storm drain after the fallout from Spatafore's execution.

Grigio, Sammy

Actor: Salvatore Piro

Can be found in episodes: "Pax Soprana"

Ran a card game for the Altieri crew that was raided by Mikey Palmice even though it was technically under Jimmy Altieri's protection.

Pitsaturo, Vincent "Vinny Pitts"

Actor: Gino Carafelli

Can be found in episodes: "Cold Cuts"

Member of Carlo Gervasi's crew who surveilled shipments that came through NJ ports.

Anastasia, Jerry

Actor: Unseen character

Referenced in: "Two Tonys"

Tony mentions Jerry Anastasia as a guy he had to buy dinner for when he was newly made.

Curto, Raymond

Actor: George Loros

Can be found in episodes: "Meadowlands", "Pax Soprana", "The Legend of Tennessee Moltisanti", "Nobody Knows Anything", "I Dream of Jeannie Cusamano", "Guy Walks into a Psychiatrist's Office...", "Proshai, Livushka", "Fortunate Son", "...To Save Us All From Satan's Power", "For All Debts Public and Private", "No Show", "Two Tonys", "Rat Pack", "Long Term Parking", "All Due Respect" and "Members Only"

Former capo in the DiMeo/Soprano crime family who was approached by Tony to replace Jackie Aprile, Sr. as Boss. Raymond demurred and advocated that Tony take over instead.

Unfortunately, he was also an FBI informant as revealed in the episode, "Proshai, Livushka." Raymond has a son with multiple sclerosis, so perhaps Ray flipped so he could stay out of jail to care for him.

Unexpectedly, Raymond died of a stroke in 2006 while ratting out Tony for his role in a murder to Agent Sanseverino. Raymond has lasted as a rat longer than anyone in the series and unlike others, was never caught or even under suspicion.

DiMeo, Rocco

Actor: Unseen character

Referenced in: "Down Neck," "Full Leather Jacket"

Rocco DiMeo was a member of the DiMeo crime family in New Jersey but lost face when Richie Aprile forcefully relieved him of his leather jacket. Richie later gave the jacket to Tony Soprano.

La Manna, Michele "Feech"

Actor: Robert Loggia

Can be found in episodes: "All Happy Families," "Where's Johnny?," "Rat Pack," and "Two Tonys."

An OG from Italy, Feech came over to America in the 1950s, ready made, and soon after arriving became involved with the DiMeo crime family, then under the leadership of boss Ercoli 'Eckley' DiMeo. By the 1970s Feech had become one of the most respected and feared capos in the DiMeo family. Not to be outdone, a young Tony Soprano and his colleague Jackie Aprile, Sr., knocked over his card game, causing their ascendancy in the organization to accelerate.

In 1984, Feech was convicted of criminal charges and in 2004, when his sentence was up, he went to see Tony Soprano, the new boss of North Jersey, to requested his card game back et cetera. Tony agreed but Feech soon started stepping on some toes. After a power struggle with Paulie Walnuts over landscaping, Feech stole cars from the daughter of a friend of the organization, at her own wedding. Tony realized that he may not be able to keep Feech on a short enough leash, so he had Christopher Moltisanti and Benny Fazio convince Feech into holding onto a stolen shipment of plasma screen televisions. When a parole officer stops by unannounced, he drags Feech back to prison for violation of parole.

Malanga, " Little Pussy"

Actor: Uncredited

Can be found in episodes: "Pilot"

Uncle Junior plans to whack Little Pussy at the restaurant owned by Tony's childhood friend Artie Bucco. To save his friend's business from the ill repute of hosting a mob hit, Tony burns down the restaurant. Six or seven years later, Junior's dementia causes him to believe that Tony is Little Pussy and he shoots Tony in the stomach.

Martin, Romeo

Actor: Unseen character

Referenced in: "The Happy Wanderer"

Former member of the DiMeo/Soprano crime family.

Sasso, Cicchi

Actor: Nick Riao

Can be found in episodes: "Down Neck"

Cicchi Sasso is Tony's father's maternal cousin. He is a former associate of the DiMeo/Soprano crime family, and was one of the mobsters meeting with Johnny Boy Soprano in a carnival at Down Neck in the 1960s. When the park was raided by police, Cicchi attempted to escape and was shot in the kneecap, which turned out for the best because it disqualified him to serve in Viet Nam.

Cippolini, Joey

Actor: Unseen character

Can be found in episodes: "D-Girl"

Christopher Moltisanti tells Jon Favreau and Amy Safir the story of a made man who recieved a blowjob off someone that he later discovered to be a tranvestite. In revenge, the mobster burnt him with acid. When Favreau steals Chris' idea and uses it in his own script, Chris exclaims "this is Joey Cippolini's story".

Anthony, Hector

Actor: Manny Siverio

Can be found in episodes: "46 Long"

Driver for Comley Trucking, accidentally killed when Special K dropped his piece in an attempted hijacking led by Brendan Filone.

Barone, Dick

Actor: Joe Lisi

Can be found in episodes: "Pilot", "House Arrest" and "The Knight in White Satin Armor"

Owned and operated the Soprano's front for legit business: Barone sanitation. Dick died in 2006 of Lou Gehrig's disease, and his funeral was attended by many members of the Soprano crime family, and watched from afar by the FBI. Dick was survived by his wife, Helen Barone, and son, Jason Barone. After his death, Barone sanitation was bought out by Lupertazzi crime family firm, Cinelli Sanitation.

Barone Sanitation

Company that serves as a front for the mob's legal activities. In 1999, the triborough towers route was being contested, and Chris shot Emil Kolar to prevent them from getting the contract.

Caputo, Vic

Actor: Joseph Leone

Can be found in episodes: "Johnny Cakes"

Vic Caputo is the manager of Caputo's poultry - a small business of which Tony is also the landlord. Vic is forced to move his business when Tony sells the property in 2006 at a high profit to a Juice Company.

Dupree, Warren

Actor: Brian Anthony Wilson

Can be found in episodes: "Fortunate Son"

Manager of a betting shop that was given to Christopher as his first source of income after becoming a made man.

La Cerva, Adriana

Actor: Drea de Mateo

One-time hostess at the mob hangout Vesuvio, niece of Jackie and Richie Aprile, and fiancée of Christopher Moltisanti, Adriana was not repulsed by mob life. Always loving and devoted to Christopher, sticking by him through his heroin addiction and even after he abuses her, she eventually flips. As it turns out, her friend Danielle was actually an FBI agent working under cover, and witness her engaging in illegal activities while running her club, the Crazy Horse. She tries unsuccessfully to get Christopher to flip and run away with her to the Witness Protection Program, but is unsuccessful. She meets her maker in 12th episode of the 5th season when Silvio shoots her for her transgressions as a rat. Tony, knowing how upset Carmela would be, doesn't tell her that Adriana flipped and was killed by Silvio. After Adriana's mother and Carmela's friend attempts suicide in the anguish over her missing daughter, Carmela attempts to get answers out of Tony but he distracts her by helping her with her spec house. At present, Adriana has been confirmed to be dead by producers even though the camera did not show her death. She is still scheduled to appear in dreams, however.

La Manna, E Gary

Actor: Michael Cavalieri

Referenced in: "Where's Johnny"

Feech La Manna's nephew who assists him in running La Manna landscaping, and father of Jimmy La Manna. La Manna Landscaping, though a legit operation, become involved in a turf war with Paulie Walnuts' legit company Vitro Gardening, and during the course of the beef, Paulie injured Gary and Jimmy La Manna. Eventually, Tony was able to broker a solution.

La Manna, Jimmy

Actor: Anthony Desio

Referenced in: "Where's Johnny", "All Happy Families..."

Feech La Manna's relative involved in running La Manna landscaping - one of Feech's legitimate businesses. Son of E Gary La Manna. However La Manna Landscaping become involved in a turf war with Paulie Walnuts' own gardening firm Vitro Gardening and Paulie injured Gary and Jimmy La Manna.

Massarone, "Black" Jack

Actor: Robert Desiderio

Can be found in episodes: "Do Not Resuscitate", "No Show", "Rat Pack"

Owner of Massarone construction, and victim of a shakedown when black protestors picketing a construction site because they thought his employment policies were racist. He paid Tony Soprano to intervene on his behalf without knowing that Tony had actually organized and incited the protest through Reverend James, Jr. Massarone construction was later involved in Soprano get-rich-quick schemes like the Esplanade project and HUD scam.

In 2004, Jack had become a federal informant and Tony realised something was wrong when Jack gave him a picture of Rat Pack at a meeting. Jack found in the trunk of his car with a golf club cover in his mouth to send a message.

Tiffen, Maurice

Actor: Vondie Curtis-Hall

Can be found in episodes: "Watching Too Much Television"

Maurice was a college friend of Ronald Zellman who in 2002, helped Tony Soprano with a scam defraudng the Housing and Urban Development committee.

Teittleman, Hillel

Actor: Sig Libowitz

Can be found in episodes: "Denial, Anger, Acceptance", "The Happy Wanderer", "Funhouse", "Luxury Lounge"

A practicing Hassidic Jew and co-owner of the Flyaway Motel. In 1999 his brother-in-law Ariel used his upcoming divorce to negotiate a 50% share in the Teitlemann's motel where he had worked for most of his life. Hillel's father Shlomo contracted the Soprano family to intimidate Ariel despite Hillel's strenuous objections. His moral compass changed course after the mob became his business partner, facilitating mob business at his hotel and selling card information to Soprano crew associate Murmur.

Antjuan

Actor: Sharif Rashed

Can be found in episodes: "46 Long"

One of Brendan Filone's goons involved in robbing Comley trucking shipments under the protection of Uncle Junior. He accompanies Brendan and Special K on a heist even after Junior had made Brendan and Chris pay tribute for robbing his trucks. He holds his gun sideways. When Special K drops his gun and the ricochet bullet kills the truck driver, Antjuan and Special K run off, leaving Brendan to face the consequences, and ultimately, be punished.

Clayborn, John

Actor: John Eddins

Can be found in episodes: "Isabella"

Junior contracted Donnie Padua to kill Tony, and Donnie in turn contracted John Clayborn, The attempt did not go well—the first one was foiled Christopher refused to move his car. The second attempt also failed when Tony saw the reflection of his would-be assassins in the SUV window, and Clayborn was accidentally shot in the head by his partner Rasheen Ray.

Curtis, Credenzo

Actor: Curtiss Cook

Can be found in episodes: "Whitecaps"

Heroin dealer contracted by Christopher Moltisanti to kill Carmine Lupertazzi on orders from Tony Soprano. Eventually, the order on the hit was aborted, and Benny Fazio killed Curtis and his partner Stanley Johnson in the Meadowlands.

Johnson, Stanley

Actor: Universal

Can be found in episodes: "Whitecaps"

Heroin dealer hired by Christopher Moltisanti to kill Carmine Lupertazzi on Tony's orders. When it was decided that the hit was unnecessary Chris lured Stanley and his partner Credenzo Curtis to a meeting in the Meadowlands to give them the rest of their payment. He had them killed by Benny Fazio and Peter "Bissel" De Rosa and an associate before they could leave.

Ray, Rasheen

Actor: Touche

Can be found in episodes: "Isabella"

Junior contracted Donnie to kill Tony and Donnie in turn subcontracted the job to him. First attempt was aborted when Christopher accidentally foiled the plan by refusing to move his car. The second attempt also failed and Rasheen accidentally shot and killed his partner John Clayborn. Tony dragged Rasheen alongside his car, and eventually let go and left Rasheen in the street.

Special K

Actor: J. D. Williams

Can be found in episodes: "46 Long"

One of Brendan Filone's partners in the attemped hijacking of a Comley Truck. Special K's contribution to the robbery was not terribly useful, as he dropped his gun and accidentally killed the driver as a result.

Ahmed

Actor: Donnie Keshawarz

Appears in: "Join the Club", "Mr. & Mrs. John Sacrimoni Request", "Luxury Lounge", "Kaisha"

Associate of Christopher. Ahmed and his friend Muhammed can often be seen hanging out at the Bing. He, along with Muhammed, also goes to Christopher for help in getting stolen credit cards and TEC-9 semi-automatic pistols.

Muhammed

Actor: Taleb Adlah

Appears in: "Join the Club", "Mr. & Mrs. John Sacrimoni Request", "Luxury Lounge", "Kaisha"

Associate of Christopher. Muhammed and his friend Ahmed can often be seen hanging out at the Bing. He, along with Ahmed, also goes to Christopher for help in getting stolen credit cards and TEC-9 semi-automatic pistols.

Aprile, Augustus "Little Auggie"

Actor: Unseen Character

Referenced in: "Employee of the Month"

Dr. Elliot Kupferberg assumed that it was he that Dr. Melfi was treating when she was actually treating Tony Soprano.

Cogo, Joseph "Joey"

Actor: David Copeland

Can be found in episodes: "Pie-O-My", "Rat Pack"

A criminal associate of Christopher who got a bad beating at the hands of Furio. Adriana La Cerva witnesses the beating.

Debbie

Actor: Karen Sillas

Can be found in episodes: "Nobody Knows Anything"

Debbie was the madam of the brothel sometimes where Raymond Curto and Detective Vin Makazian were arrested.

Giacalone, Angelo

Actor: unseen character

Referenced in: "Members Only"

Angelo Giacalone was an unseen character referenced by Ray Curto to Agent Sanseverino. In the final moments of his life, Curto implicated Tony Soprano in the murder of an Angelo Giacalone, and claimed to have Tony talking about the hit on tape.

Haydu, Barry

Actor: Tom Mason

Can be found in episodes: "For All Debts Public and Private"

Barry Haydu was the detective from the Clifton police force that investigated the murder of Dickie Moltisanti. Tony told Christopher that Haydu was actually Dickie's killer, and that he was a crooked cop/killer for hire due to overwhelming gambling debts. Dickie, according to Tony, was named a target by Jilly Ruffalo in retribution because Dickie mutilated Jilly.

Christopher broke into Haydu's home and waited for him to return from his retirement party. Despite Haydu's insistance that he hand't killed Dickie, Chris shot him using his own gun, and placed it back in his hand so it would look like a suicide.

Kamal

Actor: Homie Doroodian

Can be found in episodes: "Long Term Parking"

A drug dealer who helped Matush murder Gilbert Nieves in a dispute over drugs in 2004.

Kaplan, Eli

Actor: David Shuman

Can be found in episodes: "Members Only"

Hesh Rabkin's son-in-law who was attacked by Jimmy Lauria, a Leotardo associate, for making collections on Hesh's behalf in Leotardo territory. The Leotardo crew did not realise Eli had been acting on Hesh's behalf. Jimmy and hit Hesh and beat up Eli. Eli fled into the street and was hit by a car. He survived but had to spend time in the hospital.

Orange J

Actor: Bryan Hicks

Can be found in episodes: "A Hit is a Hit"

A member of Massive Genius' crew.

Reverend James Junior

Actor: Gregory Alan Williams

Can be found in episodes: "Do Not Resuscitate", "Proshai, Livushka", "He Is Risen"

Son of the Reverend James Senior, he asssisted Tony in organizing a protest that Tony was later paid to break up.

Kolar, Emil

Actor: Bruce Smolanoff

Can be found in episodes: "Pilot", "The Legend of Tennessee Moltisanti"

Czech-American shot three times in the head by Christopher in the back room at Satriale's. Emil's family was involved in a bidding war over garbage routes controlled by Barone Sanitation. Chris killed Emil without authorization and Big Pussy helped Chris dispose of the body so it could look like Emil disappeared. Later, Chris is haunted by Emil in his dreams, and paranoid, he and Big Pussy move the body.

Mahaffey, Alex

Actor: Michael Gaston

Can be found in episodes: "Pilot"

Involved in a scam defrauding medical insurance companies with Hesh and Tony in order to pay back gambling debt. Initially reluctant, he became convinced after Tony ran over him and broke his leg, and Hesh and Big Pussy took him to a bridge over a waterfall and implied that if he refused, they'd throw him over.

Makazian, Vin

Actor: John Heard

Can be found in episodes: "Meadowlands", "Pax Soprana", "Boca", "Nobody Knows Anything" and "The Test Dream"

Vin Makazian was a police detective on the Soprano payroll. In addition to giving information about possible indictments, he was sent by Tony to get information about Dr. Melfi when he first started therapy with her. Tony's information came to an end when Vin was arrested at a brothel along with Soprano crime family capo Raymond Curto. Vin committed suicide by jumping from a bridge, his badge pinned to his chest, shortly after his arrest.

Massive Genius

Actor: Bokeem Woodbine

Can be found in episodes: "A Hit is a Hit"

Rap star who helps Adriana in her attempts to produce a hit record for the band Visiting Day. He also asks Christopher to arrange a sit-down for Hesh so he can collect on royalties that Hesh owes a relative of his.

Gia, Matush

Actor: Nick Tarabay

Can be found in episodes: "The Telltale Moozadell", "Amour Fou" and "Long Term Parking"
An ecstasy dealer who has had some association with Soprano/DiMeo business over the years. He tried to peddle his wares at Adriana's club, but Furio and Chris threw him off the premises. Jackie Aprile Jr., however, told him that he had gotten Chris to allow him to sell drugs outside the club, but not in it. This was untrue and Matush was beaten again.

Also noteworthy: Matush was recruited as a driver in Jackie Junior's planned robbery of a card game in 2001, but he sped away as soon as he heard gunshots, leaving Dino Zerilli and Jackie Jr. to fend for themselves. Both eventually ended up dead as a result.

In 2004 Matush had returned to dealing at the Crazy Horse, and during a transaction gone awry murdered Gilbert Nieves office and recruited Adriana to help him dispose of the body. This was observed by FBI surveillance outside and was leveraged against her. Under pressure, she tried to flip Christopher, but was killed.

Melvoin, Harold

Actor: Richard Portnow

Can be found in episodes: "Boca", "Do Not Resuscitate", "The Knight in White Satin Armor", "Another Toothpick", "Christopher", "Pie-O-My", "Whoever Did This", "Calling All Cars", "Eloise", "Whitecaps", "Where's Johnny", "In Camelot", "The Test Dream"

Harold Melvoin was Junior Soprano's lawyer from 1999-2004, and allowed Junior to use his office for business while under house arrest. After he has a stroke and develops a speech impediment, Junior fires him.

Mink, Neil

Actor: David Margulies

Can be found in episodes: "Guy Walks into a Psychiatrist's Office...", "Bust Out", "House Arrest", "Funhouse", "Mergers and Acquistions" and "All Due Respect"

Tony Soprano's lawyer.

Irish, Rusty

Actor: Christopher J Quinn

Can be found in episodes: "Pax Soprana"

Drug dealer blamed for the death of a Uncle Junior's tailor's grandson since the grandson committed suicide after buying drugs from Rusty. Mikey Palmice threw Rusty off a bridge in retaliation, which upset Larry Boy Barese since Rusty was a good earner for him.

Mendez, "Yo-Yo"

Actor: Shawn McLean

Can be found in episodes: "Meadowlands"

"Yo-Yo" is a drug dealer so named because he sports a green yo yo. He pays points to Christopher until 1999, when Junior Soprano moves in on Christopher's territory and has "Yo-Yo" pay up to him instead. Even though he is in a neck brace, Chris beats "Yo-Yo" on a street corner and says if he pays points to anyone but him that he'll be giving Christ his thumbs as punishment.

Santiago, Reuben "The Cuban"

Actor: Yul Vazquez

Can be found in episodes: "Christopher"

Reuben is an associate who visits Hesh Rabkin's horses, and angers Hesh when he draws a comparison between Christopher Columbus and Hitler.

Schartz, Marty

Actor: Jerry Grayson

Can be found in episodes: "Christopher", "Eloise" and "Whitecaps"

An associate of Hesh Rabkin who organises a meeting, a night at his casino, and a helicopter ride home between Tony Soprano and Chief Doug Smith during the unrest over Christopher Columbus day.

Smith, Chief Doug

Actor: Nick Chinlund

Can be found in episodes: "Christopher"

A casino owner who isn't able to fully help Tony ease the unrest over Columbus day, but gives Tony's crew a fully comped night at his casino.

Spirodakis, Teddy

Actor: Joseph Caniano

Can be found in episodes: "Members Only"

Killed by Eugene Pontecorvo on Christopher Moltisanti's orders for not paying debts.

Tracee

Actor: Ariel Kiley

Can be found in episodes: "University"

A stripper at the Bada Bing! who became pregnant while she was with Ralph. Ralph beat Tracee to death in the Bada Bing parking lot. Tony was incensed and later, when killing Ralph, he shouted "she was an innocent creature" which may have referred to the horse Pie-Oh-My, or to Tracee.

"Juan Valdez"

Can be found in episodes: "A Hit is a Hit"

Drug dealer killed and robbed by Paulie Walnuts for operating in Soprano territory.

Valery

Actor: Vitali Baganov

Can be found in episodes: "...To Save Us All from Satan's Power", "Pine Barrens"

Valery was an associate of the Russian mob. Paulie Walnuts and Christopher Moltisanti visited him to collect his payment on behalf of Silvio, but chaos ensued and the Russian ended up seemingly dead and in the back of their trunk, awaiting disposal. They drove out to the Pine Barrens but when they arrived he was awake and had bitten through the tape they'd used for the purposes of tying him up. They then gave him a shovel with the instructions to dig his own grave, but he used it as a weapon and ran away, but not before taking a shot to the head. Amazingly, the shot didn't slow him down, and his body was never found.

Zellman, Ronald

Actor: Peter Riegert

Can be found in episodes: "Proshai, Livushka", "Employee of the Month", "Another Toothpick", "For All Debts Public and Private", "Christopher", "Watching Too Much Television"

Ronald Zellman was Assemblyman for New Jersey in 2000 and on the Soprano payroll. He eventually dated Tony's ex-comare, Irina, and though Tony publicly professed indifference, he later beat him with a belt. Although Tony and Zellman have not been shown meeting since then, Tony turned to the Zellman in 2006, therefor allowing AJ to be released from police custody following his attempt to murder Junior in retribution for his having shot Tony in the stomach.

Zucca, Annalisa

Actor: Sofia Milos

Can be found in episodes: "Commendatori", "Funhouse"

The daughter of Zi Vittorio, head of the Neapolitan famiglia in Naples, and the acting boss since her husband is serving a life sentence.

When Tony took over Junior's luxury car "export" business, he went over to visit Zi Vittorio in Naples to discuss and finalize the arrangement. When he finally meets Zi Vittorio, Tony realizes that he's a senile, wheelchair-bound old man - and it is his daughter Annalisa who runs the organization now.

Tony and Annalisa eventually work out a deal that results in Furio being sent over to the states.

Annalisa reminds Tony of Dr. Jennifer Melfi, and she appears in a dream wherein she is speaking to him in Dr. Melfi's office during a therapy session.

Pillsbury, Devin

Actor: Jessica Dunphy

Appears in: "Everybody Hurts", "Calling All Cars", "Marco Polo", "All Due Respect"

AJ's girlfriend in 2002 and or till 2004. Devin too is from a wealthy family which occasionally causes problems with her relationship with AJ.

Selgada, Blanco

Actor: Dania Ramirez

Appears in: "Kaisha"

Blanca is A.J. Soprano's girlfriend. They met when they were both working at the construction site. Blanca is older than AJ, and has a 3 year old son named Hector.

O'Brien, Hernan

Actor: Vincent Piazza

Appears in: "Johnny Cakes", "Cold Stones"

Classmate of AJ's who began accompanying him out clubbing in New York when AJ dropped out of college. Hernan uses AJ's fame as a relation of Tony's to chat up girls and bathes in the reflected glory of his minor celebrity status.

Eric DeBenedetto

Actor: Johnny Mucci

Appears in: "Mr. & Mrs. John Sacrimoni Request", "Moe N' Joe"

Johnny Sack's son-in-law.

Charlie Garepe

Actor: Jimmy Collins

Appears in: "The Test Dream"

Angelo Garepe's son.

Leotardo, Patty

Actor: Geraldine LiBrandi

Appears in: "Mayham", "Mr. & Mrs. John Sacrimoni Request", "Luxury Lounge", "Cold Stones" "Kaisha"

Patty is the wife of Lupertazzi crime family acting boss Phil Leotardo, and is close friends with most of the other mob wives.

Lupertazzi, Nicole

Actor : Allison Dunbar

Appears in: "Two Tonys", "Marco Polo", "Unidentified Black Males"

Nicole is the wife of "Little Carmine" Lupertazzi.

Millio, Gianna

Actor: Merel Julia

Appears in: "Mr. & Mrs. John Sacrimoni Request", "Luxury Lounge"

Gianna was the wife of Lupertazzi crime family capo Rusty Millio until his death in 2006.

Sacramoni, Allegra Marie

Actor: Caitlin Van Zandt

Appears in: "Mr. & Mrs. John Sacramoni Request", "Moe N' Joe" Johnny Sack's daughter, married to Eric DeBenedetto. Her wedding was rather out of the ordinary because her father, John was released from prison to attend the wedding. This meant that Allegra had to host metal detectors and US Marshals at the ceremony and reception. AT the end of the event, her father cried as he was led away and her mother fainted.

Sacramoni, Catherine

Actor: Christina Milion

Appears in: "Mr. & Mrs. John Sacramoni Request", "Moe N' Joe"

Johnny Sack's daughter. There has been some allusion to a possible eating disorder, but it is as of yet unconfirmed.

Sacramoni, Ginny

Actor: Denise Borino

Appears in: "Employee of the Month", "He Is Risen", "Army of One", "Christopher", "The Weight", "Whitecaps", "Two Tonys", "Rat Pack", "Unidentified Black Males", "All Due Respect", "Members Only", "Mr. & Mrs. John Sacramoni Request", "Moe N' Joe", "Kaisha"

Ginny is the wife of John "Johnny Sack" Sacramoni and the mother of Catherine and Allegra Marie Sacramoni. Once a lithe and fit professional dancer, Ginny became somewhat obese after having children, but her husband loves her nonetheless. Ginny's rubenesque figure has been the butt of many jokes, which once almost led to a war between her husband and Ralph Cifaretto.

Ginny turned 50 in the episode "Moe and Joe", and the mob wives were with her to celebrate. After Johnny was convicted of racketeering, Ginny had to sell her home so Janice Soprano could move in.

DeTrolio, Finn

Actor: Will Janowitz

Appears in:: "Eloise", "Whitecaps", "All Happy Families...", "Irregular Around The Margins", "Marco Polo", "Unidentified Black Males", "The Test Dream", "Members Only", "Mayham", "The Fleshy Part of the Thigh", "Mr. & Mrs. John Sacrimoni Request", "Live Free or Die", "The Ride"

Finn De Trolio is Meadow's fiancé. He is originally from Mission Viejo, CA, and is in dental school. He met Meadow Columbia University and began sharing an apartment together in her sophomore year (2002).

Noteworthy was Finn's roll in uncovering Vito as a homosexual. He told Meadow that he saw Vito give oral sex to a man at the construction site, and then Carmela insisted Meadow tell Tony, which meant that Finn was brought to Satriale's to tell basically everybody.

Hauser, Don

Actor: Kevin O'Rourke

Appears in: "Boca"

Soccer coach to the daughters of Tony, Silvio and Artie, who was well loved for his skill at getting the team to win until it was revealed that he had sex with one of the young girls on his team, prompting her to attempt suicide. Tony, after some deliberation, refrained from resorting to physical violence to avenge Ally, and the Coach was ultimately arrested.

Scangarelo, Hunter

Actor: Michelle DeCesare

Appears in: "Pilot", "Denial, Anger, Acceptance", "Meadowlands", "Boca", "Toodle Fucking-Oo" and "Mr. Ruggerio's Neighborhood"

Hunter was a school friend of Meadow Soprano, singing in the choir with Meadow and even going with her to try to get speed from Christopher in order to stay up late and study more effectively. She was accepted to Reed and visited Meadow just after she started at college.

Tannenbaum, Noah

Actor: Patrick Tully

Appears in: "Proshai, Livushka", "Fortunate Son" and "University"

African-American Jewish boyfriend of Meadow during her first year at Columbia. Upon meeting him, Tony suffers and anxiety attack.

Vandermeed, Ally

Actor: Cara Jedell

Appears in: "Boca"

Ally was a school friend of Meadow Soprano. She most notably tried to commit suicide after losing her virginity to the soccer coach. This led to his arrest for statutory rape.

Soprano, Ercoli

Actor: Unseen Character

Referenced in: "The Happy Wanderer"

Tony's uncle and Junior's brother, who lived mostly in a mental hospital due to mental retardation.

Soprano, Harpo "Hal"

Actor: Unseen Character

Referenced in: "Guy Walks Into a Psychiatrist's Office...", "Proshai, Livushka", "Cold Cuts"

Harpo is the estranged son of Janice Soprano who now lives in Montreal with his father.

Soprano, Giovanni Francis "Johnny Boy"

Actor: Joseph Siravo

Appears in: "Down Neck", "Fortunate Son", "Calling All Cars", "In Camelot", "The Test Dream"

Tony's deceased father, a former DiMeo family captain of The Soprano crew married Livia Pollio and father of Janice, Tony and Barbara. Johnny was well liked and his crew included Paulie Gualtieri and Salvatore "Big Pussy" Bonpensiero.

Johnny has only been seen in flashbacks to Tony's childhood or in Tony's dream sequences. Tony's first panic attack occured shortly after he watched Junior and his father hold down Mr. Satriali so as to cut off one of his finger.

Tony also witnessed Johnny Boy bringing Janice to carnivals on a regular basis, originally hurt that he wasn't included until he learned that mobsters brought their daughters to their meetings to serve as a cover and deflect suspicion. Johnny Boy also kept a comare named Fran Feltstein with whom he remained until his death in 1990 of emphysema.

Comàre

Comare is the Italian word for gossip, which has come to mean "girlfriend" or "mistress."

Goomara: see: comare.

La Paz, Valentina

Actor: Leslie Bega

Appears in: "Mergers and Acquisitions", "Whoever Did This", "The Strong, Silent Type", "Two Tonys", "In Camelot", "The Test Dream" and "Long Term Parking"

Originally Ralph Ciffaretto's girlfriend, she was drawn to Tony after they met at Hesh's horse stable. Over lunch, she told Tony how Ralph was very eccentric when it came to sex. The following day, they have sex in a hotel room where Valentina plays pranks on him when their lunch arrives. After she pushes Tony to make a decision about staying with his wife or being committed for her, her robe catches fire while trying to cook eggs for Tony. Tony quickly extinguishes the fire but Valentina is badly burned. Although Valentina will recover from the wounds and look normal, Tony breaks the news to her that he is going back to Carmela. Valentina lives in Fairfield in Essex County, New Jersey.

Blundetto, Kelly

Actor: Unseen Character

Referenced in: "Rat Pack", "Marco Polo", "Unidentified Black Males"

Tony Blundetto's estranged daughter.

Blundetto, Louise

Actor: Judy Del Giudice

Referenced in:"Cold Cuts"

Daughter of Pat Blundetto and cousin to Tony Soprano, Tony Blundetto and Christopher Moltisanti.

Cifaretto, Justin

Actor: Dane Curley

Appears in: "Employee of the Month, Whoever Did This"

Ralph Cifaretto's son who was hospitalized due to playing an unsupervised game with a bow and arrow. Shortly after this incident, his father was murdered.

Bonpensiero, Angie

Actor: Toni Kalem

Appears in: "Commendatori", "D-Girl", "House Arrest", "Funhouse", "Second Opinion", "Amour Fou", "For All Debts Public and Private", "Marco Polo", "Members Only", "Live Free or Die"

Angie Bonpensiero is Sal "Big Pussy" Bonpensiero's widow. They had three sons, including Kevin and Matt. Angie was unaware that her husband had flipped, and when he disappeared for a short time to get away from the heat of Soprano suspicion, she felt relieved by his absence. When he returned, he exhibited no interest in assisting her in coping with health problems that included cancer, and she considered suicide, or divorce. At Carmela's urging, Angie decided to move into a separate bedroom rather than end their marriage so as to provide a stable home for her children and avoid excommunication from the church for being divorced.

After Pussy "disappeared" for good, Tony continued to take care of Angie in her husband's absence - she bought a new car but was still vocal to Carmela about being strapped for cash, even lying to Carmela so she would tell Tony to give her more money. As punishment, Tony damaged the car and took away her allowance. Soon, Carmela finds Angie giving out free samples at the local Pathmark. Tony has since made her the manager of

Pussy's body shop, thriving in the role and buying a new Corvette to celebrate.

Bonpensiero, Edward "Duke"

Actor: Philip Larocca

Appears in: "Marco Polo"

Duke is Salvatore Bonpensiero's brother and a co-owner of the Body Shop. He runs the body shop alongside Angie Bonpensiero and helps repair Phil Leotardo's car.

Bonpensiero, Sal "Big Pussy"

Salvatore Bonpensiero started out as a cat burglar and also ran an auto body shop with his brother Edward "Duke" Bonpensiero. He was an associate of "Johnny Boy" Soprano and in the unrest of 1983 stood up for him. Bonpensiero was made some time after this and acted as a soldier in the Soprano crew from then onwards. He remained loyal to the Soprano family and backed Johnny Boy's wishes to have his son, Tony Soprano, become caporegime of the crew following Johnny Boy's death in 1986. Bonpensiero worked alongside other longtime Soprano associates Paulie "Walnuts" Gualtieri and Silvio Dante throughout his career in the Mafia.

Bonpensiero was a kind-hearted man who doted on his wife Angie and their three sons, and was a long-time friend of Tony's. However, the money he made from the mob was not enough to raise his three children and put them through college and he began trafficking in heroin on the side. Soprano, his capo, and Jackie Aprile Sr., then acting boss of the family, were aware of his sideline and urged him to stop dealing. He was caught by the FBI and given the choice of either working for them as an informant against Tony Soprano and his mob family or facing the possibility of life in prison. He agreed and was assigned FBI Agent Skip Lipari as a handler - he was revealed as an informant in the episode "Do Not Resuscitate."

In 1999 Bonpensiero was an essential part of the Soprano crew's operation and was exposed to a number of things he could have reported. When indictments were threatened he fled and burned papers in his back garden - perhaps a sign that he was not co-operating fully.

Since his return, he and wife had been having trouble and she discussed leaving him with Carmela Soprano, who dissuaded her because of their Catholicism. Angie settled for sleeping in separate bedrooms.

Upon his return from Italy, Soprano re-organized his crew - Gualtieri would be capo now that he was acting boss, Dante would become Tony's consigliere, and new addition Furio Giunta would be on an equal footing with Bonpensiero despite his years of long service. Bonpensiero was obviously distressed at the new order and openly hostile to Giunta and complained to Lipari that "this thing of ours" turned into "this thing of mine." His reservations about informing on Soprano began to dissipate.

Soprano eventually abandoned the blinding affection he held for Bonpensiero and realized his old friend's betrayal after a portentive dream where Bonpensiero appeared as a fish and told him that he had known all along. Soprano, Dante and Gualtieri confronted their former friend once they got out to sea and got him to admit that he had informed on them. Paulie takes some jewelry off of Pussy and the three bag him up, weigh him down and throw him overboard. All three have since been haunted by the memory of their old friend's murder.

Bonpensiero, Kevin

Actor : Giancarlo "John" Giunta

Appears in: "Nobody Knows Anything"

Kevin is one of Salvatore and Angie Bonpensiero's children.

Bonpensiero, Matt

Actor: Steve Porcelli

Appears in: "D-Girl"

Matt is one of Salvatore and Angie Bonpensiero's children, and a contemporary of AJ's, enlisted to help AJ realize the follies of renouncing his religion.

Dante, Gabriela

Actor: Maureen Van Zandt

Appears in: "Commendatori", "From Where To Eternity", "House Arrest", "The Knight in White Satin Armour", "Funhouse", "Proshai, Livushka", "Employee of the Month", "University", "To Save Us All From Satans Power", "Amour Fou", "Army of One", "Christopher", "The Weight", "Watching Too Much Television", "The Strong, Silent Type", "Irregular Around The Margins", "Unidentified Black Males", "Mayham", "Live Free or Die", "Moe N' Joe"

Gabriella is the wife of Soprano family soldier and consigliere Silvio Dante. They have a daughter, Heather Dante, and she is close friends with Rosalie Aprile and Carmela Soprano.

Dante, Heather

Actor: Jackie Tohn

Appears in: "Pilot" (Uncredited), "Boca"

The daughter of Silvio and Gabriella Dante, and classmate of Meadow Soprano. She knows that her father owns a strip club and disapproves.

Fazio, Benny (Sr)

Actor: Mario D'Elia

Appears in: "Luxury Lounge"

Father of Soprano crime family associate Benny Fazio.

Fazio, Connie

Actor: Judy Prianti

Appears in: "Luxury Lounge"

Mother of Soprano crime family associate Benny Fazio.

Fazio, Jen

Actor: Kristin Cerelli

Appears in: "Luxury Lounge"

Wife of Soprano crime family associate Benny Fazio.

Gualtieri, Maria Nuccia

Actor: Frances Ensemplare

Appears in: "Army of One", "Mergers and Acquistions", "Whoever Did This", "Eloise", "Whitecaps", "Where's Johnny?", "The Fleshy Part of the Thigh" The Ride

"Nucci" is known as Paulie Walnuts' elderly mother who was placed in the Green Grove Retirement Community shortly after Livia Soprano moved in. Her old friends, Cookie Cirillo and Minn Matrone snubbed her and excluded her from card games, so she took to her room and became depressed. Angry, Paulie badly beat Cookie's son and later killed Minn Matrone for her cash.

Much later, Paulie learns on his Aunt Dottie's deathbed that Dottie is his real mother and that Nucci adopted him to spare Dottie embarassment and save the family honor. When Paulie hears this, he refuses to attend Dottie's funeral or pay for Nucci's bbills at Green Grove. Later, however, they reconnected and reconciled.

Jim, aka "Johnny Cakes"

Actor: John Costelloe

Appears in: Live Free or Die, Luxury Lounge, Johnny Cakes, The Ride, Moe n' Joe, and Cold Stones.

Jim (also known as "Johnny Cakes" for a dish he serves at the diner he owns) was Vito Spatafore's gay lover when Vito was on the lam and living in Vermont to escape the fate that awaited him in New Jersey. Ultimately, although he and Jim moved in together and seemed to get along quite well, Vito was homesick for his family. He left for New Jersey and Jim never saw him nor heard from him again.

Palmice, JoJo

Actor: Michelle Santopietro

Appears in: "Nobody Knows Anything", "I Dream of Jeannie Cusamano", "Pie-O-My"

JoJo was the wife of Mikey Palmice, and mother of Francis-Albert and Michael Jr., but was widowed when he was killed in 1999 for his role in the attempt on Tony's life..

Parisi, Donna

Actor: Anna Mancini
Appears in: "The Weight", "Watching Too Much Television" and "Rat Pack"

Donna is the wife of Soprano soldier Pasquale "Patsy" Parisi. Though he has been with the mob for a long time, she does not seem to be close to the rest of the mob wives.

Pontecorvo, Ally

Actor: Grace Van Patten

Appears in: "Members Only", "Join the Club"

Deanne and Eugene Pontecorvo's daughter. Younger sister of Robby Pontecorvo.

Pontecorvo, Deanna

Actor: Suzanne DiDonna

Appears in: "Members Only", "Join the Club"

Eugene Pontecorvo's wife until widowed by his suicide in 2006. Upon his death and dispersal of his estate, Deanna left for Florida. When her husband was alive, Tony refused his request to retire, and so did the FBI.

Pontecorvo, Robby

Actor: Thomas Russo

Appears in: "Members Only", "Join the Club"

Deanne and Eugene Pontecorvo's son.

Spatafore, Franscesca

Actor: Paulina Gerzon

Appears in: "Mayham", "Mr. & Mrs. John Sacrimoni Request", "Live Free or Die", "Luxury Lounge", "Johnny Cakes", "Cold Stones"

Francesa Spatafore is the daughter of Vito Spatafore and Marie Spatafore and the younger sister of Vito Spatafore, Jr.

Spatafore, Marie

Actor: Elizabeth Bracco

Appears in: "Mayham", "Mr. & Mrs. John Sacrimoni Request", "Live Free or Die", "Luxury Lounge", "Johnny Cakes", "Cold Stones"

Marie Spatafore is the wife of Vito Spatafore and mother of their two children Vito, Jr. and Francesca. She is also a cousin of Phil Leotardo. Marie realizes that something is wrong with her husband when he frequently goes out late under the auspices of making collections, however, she remains loyal to him. She refuses to discuss her sex life when Vito's mob associates come looking for him, and advocates on his behalf.

When he is killed, however, she silently endures gossip about her sex life with her husband, and speculation that he was killed because he was a sinner.

Spatafore, Vito (Jr.)

Actor: Frank Borrelli

Appears in: "Members Only", "Mr. & Mrs. John Sacrimoni Request", "Live Free or Die", "Luxury Lounge", "Johnny Cakes", "Cold Stones"

Vito Spatafore, Jr. is the son of Vito Spatafore and Marie Spatafore and the brother of Francesca Spatafore. Vito went on the lam after associates were making collections at a gay bar and saw him there, taking on a fake identity in a small Vermont town and even taking on a male lover. When he returned, he was executed for his sexual predilection, leaving a wife and small children behind.

Tom Giglione

Actor: Ed Vassalo

Appears in: "Guy Walks into a Psychiatrist's Office...", "The Happy Wanderer", "Funhouse", "Proshai, Livushka", "Where's Johnny?", "In Camelot", "Mayham", "Moe N' Joe"

Barbara's husband and Tony and Janice's brother-in-law.

Sacramoni, Johnny "Sack"

The boss of the New York family, Johnny Sack is known for his intelligence and experience in the business.
Though not a member of Tony's crew, Johnny has been an important ally of Tony's for some time. When then-underboss Johnny and Ginny moved from New York to New Jersey, Johnny assured Tony that he wanted to be closer to his wife's family, not Tony's business. In the later part of the series, Johnny was hauled off by the Feds while Tony made a run for it and escaped Now in the joint longterm, Johnny has lost the respect of many of his crew members.

Rocco

Associate of Johnny Soprano's who asked him to come to Reno to run a supper club. Ultimately, Livia refused and Johnny couldn't take the offer to get out of crime and go legit.

Zucco, Victorio

Senile Don of the Family in Naples, he is boss in name only.

Zucco, Mario

Breifly the boss of the Zucco family, now incarcerated.

LaPenna, Jason

Dr. Melfi's college-age son.

LaPenna, Richard

Dr. Melfi's ex husband.

Soprano, Janice

Janice is Tony's big sister, the eldest child of Livia and Johnny Boy Soprano. She left New Jersey in her twenties and lived in San Francisco and then Los Angeles, where she joined an ashram. While living in the ashram, she worked for a moving company and changed her name to Parvati Wasatch. When she got bored with that, she traveled around Europe, where she married a French Canadian named Eugene, and had a son they named Harpo. Eventually, Parvati went to Seattle, and worked in a coffeehouse. She left after convincing a Workers Comp board that she had developed Carpal Tunnel Syndrome from operating the steamed milk machine.

Parvati was living off her disability checks when word reached her of Livia's stroke, and she returned to New Jersey to look after her invalid mother. While there, she struck up a new relationship with an old flame, Richie Aprile. The relationship came to an abrupt end when he hit her and she calmly retrieved a gun from a kitchen cabinet and shot him to death. Shortly thereafter Tony sent her back to Seattle.

But when Livia died, Janice returned home to stay. After being put in the hospital by the Russian mob for stealing her mother's former CNA's prosthetic leg, Janice found Christ.

Her Christianity did not stop her from engaging in more premarital sex, and she carried on a brief but torrid affair with

Ralph Cifaretto, but ending it when Bobby Baccilieri became widowed. When she got arrested for assaulting the mother of a her stepson's colleague on the pee wee soccer team, Bobby sent her to anger management counseling. She showed imrovement until Tony taunted her about her long-estranged son, asking: "What's French-Canadian for 'I grew up without a mother?'""

Capuano, Fred

Late owner of Green Groves. After caught spreading rumors that Tony was going to suffocate his mother with a pillow, his toupee and car are found by the side of a road.

Isabella

Tony conjures her up as a dream, which Dr. Melfi theorizes is an expression of his desire for a mother figure.

Bones, Jimmy

A friend of Pussy Bonsapiero's and an Elvis impersonator, he sees Pussy with the feds. Worried, Pussy bludgeons him to death with a hammer.

Aprile, Jackie (Jr.)

Son of Jackie Sr, who defies his father's wishes that he not get involved in the mob. After he attempts to knock over a card game

Kupferberg, Eliot

Dr. Melfi's own psychiatrist.

Fazio, "Little" Benny

Actor: Max Casella

Benny began his affiliation with the crew by driving for Tony, but soon became eager to move up in the ranks. He hung around Christopher, hoping that Chris' seniority might rub off on him and it eventually paid off when he and Christopher's pulled a heist at Rutgers University.

He fell out of favor and overstepped his bounds when he got involved in a credit card scam, using his girlfriend to swipe credit card numbers from Vessuvio. This business venture led to the closure of Vessuvio's Amex account, and an intervention from Tony which did not end well for Little Benny.

Germani, " Little" Paulie

Actor: Carl Capotorto

Nephew of Paulie Walnuts who hopes to move up in the organization by keeping his nose clean and doing what he's told.

Trillo, Gloria

Actor : Annabella Sciorra

Appears in: "He Is Risen", "The Telltale Moozadell", "Pine Barrens", "Amour Fou", "Everybody Hurts", "Calling All Cars", and "The Test Dream"

Gloria Trillo was a car salesperson for Globe Motors who met Tony in the lobby of Dr. Melfi's. Tony's romance with her was short lived, ending after she exhibited bouts of manic depression that culminated in her having the gall to talk to Carmela.

Eventually, her mental instability gets the best of her, and she hangs herself shortly after her breakup with Tony.

Giunta, Furio

Actor: Frederico Castelluccio.

Furio Giunta was the one member of the Soprano crew who was actually born and raised in Italy. When in Naples on business, Tony cut a deal that included bringing Furio to New Jersey to be in his crew.
He thrived stateside until he fell in love with Carmela Soprano. Realizing he had to stay away from her to stay alive, he put his house on the market, and left for Italy.

Skiff, Julianna

Actor: Julianna Margulies

Appears in: "Johnny Cakes", "The Ride", "Kaisha"

Real estate agent working for Century 21 who ended up closing a sale with Tony. Tony makes a pass at her, which at first she accepts but then abruptly declines, telling him she's engaged. After she later makes a pass at Tony and Tony declines, she goes to an AA Meeting and meets Christopher Moltisanti.

Despite warnings from both their sponsors, and the fact that Chris has a pregnant wife at home, Christopher and Julianna began a relationship that Christopher eventually revealed to Tony. Together, they jumped back down the hole of addiction.

Parisi, Pasquale "Patsy"

Actor Dan Grimaldi

A soldier in the Soprano Crew, Patsy had an identical twin, Phil (AKA Philly Spoons) Parisi, who unfortunately defied Tony and paid for it with his life. Patsy merely peed in Tony's pool in retribution, unable to touch a made man without dying himself. Eventually his grief subsided but was once again thrown a curveball when Christopher was made Capo of the Gualtieri crew even though Patsy felt more qualified.

At first he was disrespectful to Chris, but as of Season Six, he seems to have gotten over it.

Cifaretto, Ralph

Actor: Joe Pantoliano

Ralph Cifaretto was a member of Tony Soprano's crime family, spending time out of state but returning after Richie Aprile died. His most noteworthy moments include beating a stripper to death when she was pregnant with his child, and burning down a stable with his racehorse in it.

He had a short relationship with Rosalie Aprile, ordering the death of her son while they were still together, and then moved on to Janice Soprano, who spilled the beans to Tony about his penchant for masochism.

His son Justin was hospitalized after playing with a bow and arrow, and shortly thereafter, Tony killed him in a rage after discovering that Ralph had purposefully burned Pie-Oh-My, the racehorse, to death in order to get insurance money.

Intintola, Father Phil

Actor: Paul Schulze (1999-present), Michael Santoro (Pilot Only)

Appears in: "Pilot", "College", "Pax Soprana", "Isabella", "I Dream of Jeannie Cusamano", "Another Toothpick", "Christopher", "Mergers and Acquisitions", "Whoever Did This", "Sentimental Education", "In Camelot", "Marco Polo", "Mayham", "Mr. & Mrs. John Sacrimoni Request"

A local priest who makes Tony feel uncomfortable because he is overly fond of Carmela. Carmela claims that Father Phil is a spiritual guide to becoming a better Catholic.

Gualtieri, Peter Paul "Walnuts"

Peter Paul Gualtieri, or Paulie Walnuts, was into crime from a very young age, dropping out of school and spending time in juvenile hall. At seventeen, he joined Johnny Boy Soprano's crew.

He's very superstitous, doesn't shrink from violence, has a bad temper, and has never been married.

Paulie eventually learns that Nucci, the woman he believed was his mother, was actually his aunt, and that his real mother was his dying Aunt Dotty, a nun. Shortly after learning the truth about his family, he developed prostate cancer, and as of season six, is battling the disease.

Musto, Vic

Actor: Joe Penny

Appears in: "Bust Out", "The Knight in White Satin Armor"

Vic is the brother-in-law David Scatino and a decorator that Carmela Soprano hired to wallpaper the dining room in her home.. Carmela and Vic once kissed in the bathroom, and plan to meet for lunch, but he cancels his lunchdate.

Wegler, Robert

Actor: David Strathairn

Appears in: "Cold Cuts", "Sentimental Education", "All Happy Families..."

Robert Wegler was AJ's high school guidance counselor, and had a relationship with Carmela Soprano while she was separated from Tony. He ended the relationship because he wrongly suspected that Carmela was using him to improve AJ's grades.

Arkaway, Aaron

Actor: Turk Pipkin

Appears in: "He Is Risen", "The Telltale Moozadell", "...To Save Us All From Satan's Power", "The Fleshy Part of the Thigh"

Boyfriend of Janice Soprano in 2001, a devout fundamentalist Christian and a narcoleptic.

Bucco, Art

Actor: John Ventimiglia

Husband to Charmaine Bucco and father of Chiara Bucco, Melissa Bucco and Arthur "Art" Bucco III.

Artie is a longtime childhood friend of Tony Soprano that owns an upscale Italian restaurant called Vesuvio. At the behest of his wife, he does his best not to get involved with Tony's illegal dealings, despite many offers from Tony. While he and his wife are separated, he tries his hand at loan sharking, but fails miserably, becoming indebted to Tony. Tony offers to bail him out in exchange for Artie forgiving Tony's $6,000 tab at his restaurant, and the two friends end up not speaking for some time over the conflict.

Eventually, Artie gets back together with his wife Charmaine, and they return to managing the restaurant together. The end of season six sees them experiences hard times with their business due to lack of patrons, and Artie revisits his managerial style.

Bucco, Charmaine

Actor: Kathrine Narducci

Old friend of Carmela and Tony's, married to Artie Bucco, and mother of Chiara Bucco, Melissa Bucco and Arthur "Art" Bucco III. Although old friends with the Sopranos, Charmaine resents their lifestyle and is wary of Tony, cautioning her husband to stay far away from anything Tony offers that could even remotely be considered illegal. She and her husband separate breifly, but as of Season Six, reconcile.

Cusamano, Jeannie

Actor: Saundra Santiago

Appears in: "A Hit is a Hit", "I Dream of Jeannie Cusamano", "Full Leather Jacket", "Mr. Ruggerio's Neighborhood"

Dr. Cusamano's wife, and neighbor to the Sopranos. She is friendly with Carmela, but intimidated by the Soprano family's mob connections.

Cusamano, Joan

Actor: Saundra Santiago

Can be seen in: "Full Leather Jacket".

Twin sister to Jeannie Cusamano that Carmela intimidated into writing a letter of recommendation for Meadow.

Fanny

Actor: Marcia Haufrecht

Appears in: "46 Long" and "Proshai, Livushka"

A friend of Livia Soprano. Livia accidentally hit her with her car after driving her home, breaking her hip.

Felstein, Fran

Actor: Polly Bergen

Appears in: "In Camelot"

Fran was the longterm Comare of Johnny Boy Soprano until his death in 1986. Tony met Fran at his father's graveside and Tony got to know her a bit. Fran appealed to Tony to help her get her promised share in a go-karting track that was co-owned by Johnny Boy with Hesh Rabkin and Phil Leotardo. He did so, but eventually broke off the friendship when he became resentful upon realizing that his father was with Fran when he was needed at home.

Piocosta, George

Actor: Sal Petraccione

Appears in: "Meadowlands" and "Fortunate Son"

George is the father of AJ Soprano's one time friend, Jeremy Piocosta and an acquaintance of Tony Soprano. Initially, George seemed very intimidated by Tony Soprano, but later gets over it when he watches AJ's high school football game alongside Tony.

Sanfillipo, Roberta "Bobbi"

Actor: Robyn Peterson

Appears in: "Boca"

Roberta was a long-term friend/comare of Junior Soprano.. Roberta and Junior's sixteen-year relationship ended in 1999 when Bobbi defied Junior's insistance that she keep his sexual skills as a on the down low, and told her pedicurist that Junior went down on her. The pedicurist told another client who told Carmela, who in turn told Tony. Tony made dirty jokes at the golf course to taunt Junior, and Junior broke up with Bobbi by smashing a lemon meringue pie in her face.

Scatino, David

Actor: Robert Patrick

Appears in: "The Happy Wanderer", "Bust Out", "Funhouse"

David Scatino is a childhood friend of Tony Soprano, and owner of Ramsey Sports and Outdoors. Tony allowed David to join in a high stakes poker game with full knowledge that David had few assets and little know-how, and David quickly became heavily indebted to Tony. Tony took over his business, and took David's son's car, which he gave to Meadow, causing potential awkwardness because she had been friends with David's son Eric. After losing his business, his home, and his marriage, Dave checked into a mental facility.

Aprile, Rosalie

Actor: Sharon Angela

Rosalie is the widow of Jackie Aprile, Sr., and the mother of Kelli and the late Jackie, Jr.. Two years after her husband died of cancer, she began seeing Ralph Cifaretto, who had been a friend of her late husband's when they were growing up.

Unbeknownst to Rosalie, it was Ralph who ordered her son's death after he tried to knock over a card game and it went awry. Vito Spatafore shot her son in the back of the head, and the story fed to Rosalie and the mob wives was that Jackie Jr. was killed by drug dealers.

Following her son's death, Rosalie became extremely depressed and Ralph began an affair with Janice Soprano.

Baccalieri, Bobby Jr.

Actor: Angelo Massagli

Appears in: "For All Debts Public and Private", "Christopher", "The Weight", "Pie-O-My", "Calling All Cars", "Rat Pack", "Where's Johnny?", "Sentimental Education", "In Camelot", "Cold Cuts", "The Test Dream", "The Ride", "Moe N' Joe", "Kaisha"

Son of Bobby and the late Karen Baccalieri, brother of Sophia Baccalieri, stepson of Janice Soprano-cum-Baccalieri. Bobby Jr.'s mother died in a car accident in 2002, often bullied by the older AJ.

Baccalieri, Karen

Actor: Christine Pedi

Appears in: "For All Debts Public and Private" and "Christopher"

Bobby Baccalieri's late wife who died in a car accident in 2002. They had two children, Bobby Jr. and Sophia. Bobby blamed himself for Karen's death as he refused to run certain errands and she died doing them herself.

Baccalieri, Sophia

Actor: Lexie Sperduto (2002) and Miryam Coppersmith (2004-present)

Appears in: "For All Debts Public and Private", "Christopher", "Pie-O-My", "Calling All Cars", "Two Tonys", "Rat Pack", "Where's Johnny?", "Sentimental Education", "In Camelot", "Cold Cuts", "The Test Dream", "The Ride", "Kaisha"

Daughter of Bobby and Karen Baccalieri, stepdaughter of Janice Soprano-cum-Baccaliere, sister of Bobby Baccalieri, Jr. Sophia's mother died in a car accident in 2002 Sophia's father remarried Janice Soprano became Sophia's stepmother.

Blundetto, Justin

Actor: Dennis Aloia

Appears in: "All Happy Families...", "Sentimental Education", "Marco Polo", "The Test Dream"

Tony Blundetto's son, not estranged.

Cubitoso, Frank (FBI Chief)

Actor: Frank Pellegrino

Appears in: "I Dream of Jeannie Cusamano", "The Knight in White Satin Armor", "Funhouse", "Mr. Ruggerio's Neighborhood", "Another Toothpick", "...To Save Us All From Satan's Power", "The Army of One", "No Show", "Watching Too Much Television", "Rat Pack", "Irregular Around the Margins", "Long Term Parking"

FBI chief of New Jersey division who is determined to indict Tony Soprano, and pressures Adriana to wear the wire that ultimately causes her death.

Agent who handled Eugene Pontecervo prior to his suicide.

Grasso, Frank (FBI Agent)

Actor: Frank Pando

Appears in: "The Legend of Tennessee Moltisanti", "I Dream of Jeannie Cusamano", "D-Girl", "Mr. Ruggerio's Neighborhood", "Proshai, Livushka", "The Army of One", "Whoever Did This", "Whitecaps", "Rat Pack", "Irregular Around the Margins", "All Due Respect"

An FBI agent who handled flipped mob capo Raymond Curto.

Harris, Dwight (FBI Agent)

Actor: Matt Servitto

Appears in: "The Legend of Tennessee Moltisanti", "I Dream of Jeannie Cusamano", "Bust Out", "House Arrest", "Funhouse", "Mr. Ruggerio's Neighborhood", "Another Toothpick", "...To Save Us All From Satan's Power", "The Army of One", "No Show", "Christopher", "Pie-O-My" "Watching Too Much Television", "Whoever Did This", "Whitecaps" "Rat Pack", "Irregular Around the Margins", "Long Term Parking", "Members Only", "Join the Club", "Kaisha"

FBI agent specializing in investigating the DiMeo crime family and their associates.

Lipari, Skip (FBI Agent)

Actor: Louis Lombardi

Appears in: "Do Not Resuscitate", "Commendatori", "Big Girls Don't Cry", "D-Girl", "From Where to Eternity", "Bust Out", "The Knight In White Satin Armor", "Funhouse", "Mr. Ruggerio's Neighborhood"

FBI agent who handled Big Pussy Bonpensiero.

Marquez, Joe (FBI Agent)

Actor: Gary Perez

Appears in: "House Arrest", "Mr. Ruggerio's Neighborhood"

Agent Harris' partner from 2000 to 2001.

Sanseverino, Robyn (FBI Agent)

Actor: Karen Young

Appears in: "Pie-O-My" "Watching Too Much Television", "The Strong, Silent Type", "Whitecaps" "Rat Pack", "Where's Johnny?", "Irregular Around the Margins", "Unidentifed Black Males", "Cold Cuts", "Long Term Parking", "Members Only"

An FBI agent who handled Adriana La Cerva after she became unresponsive and angry with Agent Ciccerone.

Waldrup, Deborah Ciccerone (FBI Agent)

Actor: Fairuza Balk (scenes deleted), Lola Glaudini

Appears in: "The Army of One", "For All Debts Public and Private", "No Show", "Christopher", "Pie-O-My", "Watching Too Much Television", "Rat Pack", "Irregular Around the Margins"

A special agent who went undercover as "Danielle" and ultimately gathered enough evidence for the FBI to persuade Adriana to flip.

April, Jackie Jr

Played by Jason Cerbone

Son of the late Jackie Aprile who briefly dated Meadow. Defying his father's wish that he not become involved in crime, Jackie participated in the attempted robbery of made man Eugene Pontecorvo, and paid for it with his life when Vito Spatafore shot him in the back of the head.

List of Rats

- Fabian "Febby" Petrulio aka Fred Peters: whacked by Tony Soprano

- Jimmy Altieri (capo, DiMeo family): whacked by Silvio, found with a rat stuffed in his mouth.

- Sal "Big Pussy" Bonpensiero (soldier, DiMeo family): whacked by Tony Soprano, Silvio Dante, and Paulie Gualtieri

- Adriana La Cerva (fiancée of Christopher Moltisanti): Whacked by Silvio

- Raymond Curto (capo, DiMeo family): Died of a stroke.

- Jack Massarone (business associate, construction): whacked.

- Jimmy Petrille (consigliere, Lupertazzi family): at large

- Eugene Pontecorvo (soldier, DiMeo family): hung himself

List of DiMeo Family Associates

Soprano/Gualtieri crew Members and Affiliates
- Alfie
- Perry Annunziata
- Matthew Bevilaqua
- Pat Blundetto
- Salvatore "Big Pussy" Bonpensiero
- Corky Caporale
- Frankie Cortese
- Peter "Bissel" De La Rosa
- Cary DiBartolo
- Benny Fazio
- Brendan Filone
- "Little Paulie" Germani
- Gaetano Giarizzo
- Burt Gervasi
- Sean Gismonte
- Furio Giunta
- Georgie
- Corky Ianucci
- Christopher Moltisanti
- Richard "Dickie" Moltisanti
- Pasquale "Patsy" Parisi
- Fabian "Febby" Petrullio
- Giovanni "Johnny Boy" Soprano
- James "Murmur" Zancone

Aprile crew associates

- Jackie Aprile, Jr.
- Richie Aprile
- Gigi Cestone
- Ralph Cifaretto
- "Big" Frank Cippolina
- Peter "Beansie" Gaeta
- Dante Greco
- Bobby Coniglio
- Corky DiGioia
- Dogsy
- Donny K
- Jason Molinaro
- Eugene Pontecorvo
- Carlo Renzi
- Bryan Spatafore
- Vito Spatafore
- "Sunshine"
- Dino Zerilli

Junior Soprano/Bacala crew associates

- Bobby Baccalieri
- Robert "Bobby" Baccalieri, Sr.
- Thomas "Tommy" Di Palma
- Salvatore "Mustang Sally" Intile
- Murf Lupo
- Donnie Paduana

- Phillip "Philly Spoons" Parisi
- Beppy Scerbo
- Charles "Chucky" Signore
- Barese crew associates
- Albert "Ally Boy" Barese
- Lorenzo "Larry Boy" Barese

Altieri/Gervasi crew associates
- Jimmy Altieri
- Tony Blundetto
- Terry Doria
- Carlo Gervasi
- Sammy Grigio
- Vincent "Vinny Pitts" Pitsaturo

Other members and associates
- Jerry Anastasia
- Raymond Curto
- Rocco DiMeo
- Michele "Feech" La Manna
- "Little Pussy" Malanga
- Romeo Martin
- Cicchi Sasso
- Joey Cippolini

Legit Business Associates and Covers
- Harold Melvoin
- Neil Mink

- Hector Anthony
- Dick Barone
- Vic Caputo
- Warren Dupree
- E. Gary La Manna
- Jimmy La Manna
- Jack Massarone
- Hillel Teittleman
- Shlomo Teittleman
- Maurice Tiffen

Contracted Hit Men
- Antjuan
- John Clayborn
- Credenzo Curtis
- Stanley Johnson
- Rasheen Ray
- Special K

Other associates
- Ahmed and Muhammad
- Augustus "Little Auggie" Aprile
- Joseph "Joey" Cogo
- Debbie
- Angelo Giacalone
- Barry Haydu
- Kamal
- Eli Kaplan

- Orange J
- Reverend James Junior
- Emil Kolar
- Alex Mahaffey
- Vin Makazian
- Massive Genius
- Matush Gia
- Herman "Hesh" Rabkin
- Rusty Irish
- "Yo-Yo" Mendez
- Reuben "The Cuban" Santiago
- Marty Schartz
- Chief Doug Smith
- Teddy Spirodakis
- Tracee
- "Juan Valdez"
- Valery
- Ronald Zellman
- Annalisa Zucca

INDEX

ADHD 15
Barone sanitation 76
Blockbuster 30
Body Shop 117
cancer..... 21, 37, 43, 61, 116, 139, 146
capo. 43, 54, 62, 65, 67, 70, 93, 106, 118, 119, 150, 155
Cinelli Sanitation 76
Columbia University 14, 109
Crazy Horse 78, 94
DiMeo 12, 25, 40, 42, 50, 51, 57, 67, 70, 71, 72, 73, 74, 94, 113, 151, 155, 159
Down Neck... 26, 71, 74, 113
ducks 16
EMT 48
FBI ... 12, 17, 25, 28, 67, 71, 76, 78, 94, 118, 126, 149, 150, 151, 152
Florida.....................126
Flyaway Motel.....23, 81
gambling 22, 88, 92
Green Grove. 15, 19, 66, 123, 124
heroin..... 17, 28, 47, 78, 118
hijacking 34, 75, 85

Hollywood........... 17, 53
homosexuality 68
HUD 44, 57, 80
La Manna landscaping 79
Leotardo 34, 35, 39, 49, 90, 105, 117, 128, 144
Los Angeles 132
Lupertazzi ... 26, 34, 76, 83, 84, 105, 106, 155
Maine 25
Massarone construction 80
Massarone Construction 31
New Jersey...19, 25, 36, 61, 71, 101, 114, 124, 130, 132, 136, 149
panic attack............ 113
Ramsey Sports and Outdoors 31, 146
rehab 17, 30
Rutgers University..134
San Francisco.......... 132
Scatino family 31
Triborough Towers Garage is................ 20
Vermont 124, 129
Visiting Day . 27, 28, 93
Vitro Gardening 79
Witness Protection Program 78

www.ingramcontent.com/pod-product-compliance
Ingram Content Group UK Ltd.
Pitfield, Milton Keynes, MK11 3LW, UK
UKHW041418180426
11947UKWH00007B/197